PRACTICAL WISDOM
TO REIGN IN LIFE

A Study of the Book of James

PRACTICAL WISDOM TO REIGN IN LIFE

A Study of the Book of James

DON GRIFFIN

LAURUS BOOKS

Unless otherwise notated, all Scripture references are from the NEW AMERICAN STANDARD BIBLE® (NASB), Copyright ©1960, 1962, 1963, 1968, 1971, 1972, 1973, 1975, 1977, 1995 by The Lockman Foundation. Used by permission.

Scripture quotations marked NKJV are taken from the New King James Version®. Copyright © 1982 by Thomas Nelson, Inc. Used by permission. All rights reserved.

Scripture references marked KJV are from the King James Version of the Holy Bible, available in the Public Domain.

PRACTICAL WISDOM TO REIGN IN LIFE
A Study of the Book of James

By Don Griffin

Copyright © 2019 by Donald Griffin

All rights reserved. This book is protected under the copyright laws of the United States of America. This book may not be copied or reprinted for commercial gain or profit. The use of short quotations or occasional page copying for personal or group study is permitted and encouraged. Permission will be granted on request.

Paperback: ISBN: 978-1-943523-62-7

Mobi (Kindle): ISBN: 978-1-943523-63-4

ePub (iBooks, Nook): ISBN: 978-1-943523-64-1

Published by LAURUS BOOKS

Author Email: don@griffinagency.com

LAURUS BOOKS
A DIVISION OF THE LAURUS COMPANY, INC.
www.TheLaurusCompany.com

This book may be ordered in paperback format from the following: www.TheLaurusCompany.com, Amazon.com, BarnesandNoble.com, and most other retailers around the world. May also be available in formats for electronic readers from their respective stores. Also available to retailers in Spring Arbor.

INTRODUCTION

The letter of James to the Church is one of the most unique and, to some, controversial letters of the New Testament. Often referred to as the "Proverbs of the New Testament," it is full of wisdom for everyday life.

Some theologians view James' epistle as opposition to the letters of Paul. Others, including Martin Luther, considered it to be a "good book," but they were also of the opinion that it was not the work of an apostle (messenger). Therefore, they did not believe that it should be a part of the Holy Scriptures. Luther and many other church leaders were in agreement that James' epistle provided many areas of sound teaching and instruction for good behavior, but here was the difficulty: they also believed that James erred by teaching that we are justified by works. James does indeed teach that we are justified by works, but he does not teach that our works are our justification for salvation, and there is the huge difference. This we do know: God, in His sovereignty, has decreed that the Epistle of James is His inspired Word, or it would not be a part of the sixty-six books of the Bible, and because it is, we know that it is devoid of error, as is all Scripture. We simply need revelation to understand correctly what has been written.

James is *not* in opposition to Paul's teaching that it is grace plus faith, devoid of work, that justifies us before God. Paul and James are both absolutely correct in what they are teaching, but we need to clearly understand that while Paul is teaching that grace alone is how we receive salvation, James is teaching that grace has also empowered us to work out our salvation. Paul wrote in Philippians 2:12, *"work out your salvation with fear and trembling."* We could say it this way, "We should take every opportunity to use the awesome and supernatural gifts we received at salvation and not be guilty of sitting idly on the sidelines." James did not say, "Work for your salvation." He said, "Work out your salvation."

It is abundantly clear that Paul's teaching of Grace does not in any way contradict James' teaching of Works. God has removed the veil to enable us to see clearly that the letter of James and the letters of Paul are in perfect harmony with each other. James is adamantly saying that our works are the "**evidence**" of our salvation, while the Apostle Paul is saying that grace plus faith, devoid of any works, is the "**root**" of our salvation. A healthy tree must have a healthy root, which allows it to eventually produce good fruit. Both messages are in complete harmony with each other and fit perfectly together in Scripture. Jesus taught the parable of the talents to show us that we are expected to produce good fruit. When we stand before the Bema Seat of Christ, we will receive or lose rewards based on what we have done with our salvation. An apple tree produces apples because it was created to produce apples. Referring to Christians, Jesus said, *"You will know them by their fruits"* (Matthew 7:16).

SUMMARY

The central theme of every Book of the Bible is Jesus, whether hidden or exclaimed, but there is also a personal message in each Book that Jesus Himself wants to convey to every Christian. The first and foremost theme is that Christ Jesus is the Sufficient One, the Provision for every part and portion of our lives. He also wants to convey to every Christian that He is the Good Shepherd who watches continuously over His children. Finally, He wants to convey to His children that He loves us where we are, but He is unwilling to leave us where we are.

Different teachers and commentators will not always agree on the central theme of the Book of James, and that is okay. When we sit down at God's table, we must learn to eat and glean the food that God wants us to digest. The message that God has written for you in the Book of James will not always be what the Lord desires to teach someone else. As we journey through this wonderful study, we will find many important messages from which everyone can glean, such as justification, faith and works, the power of our tongue, and exemplary Christian behavior. Each of these subjects is supernaturally beneficial, but there is one theme not yet mentioned that blends everything together. Jesus talked about this important virtue when He said, *"No one, after putting his hand to the plow and looking back, is fit for the Kingdom of God"* (Luke 9:62). It is the virtue of being **single-minded**. A single-minded person is one who refuses to be conformed to the wisdom of the world.

James offers Christians a choice between the wisdom of God and the wisdom of the world, continually driving home the point that mixing the wisdom of God with the wisdom of the world is being "double-minded." He points out that God only sends good, not judgment, into our lives. He moves from subject to subject on matters of Christian living and Christian behavior, causing us to examine our own level of Christian maturity.

If we fail to grasp the central theme that James is presenting, we can easily conclude that James' letter is all about law and works. This seemed to be the mindset of Martin Luther, but it is not in any way a judgment or condemnation of his views. Martin Luther had an extraordinary perception of the Gospel of Grace for the time and cultural environment in which he lived. In fact, many in the Roman Church considered him a type of heretic for his teaching of grace. Thankfully, God has chosen to give the present-day Church an even greater revelation of His unmerited love and grace. (See Daniel 12:4.)

A thorough study of this great epistle will present three

spiritual absolutes that will challenge the way we see ourselves. It will also cause every serious reader to re-evaluate their personal relationship with Christ.

First: James will reveal **who we are**, our true identity, based on our actions and reactions to the ups and downs of life.

Second: James will reveal **Whose we are** (true bond-servants?). Proverbs 22:1 reminds us that *"A good name is to be more desired than great wealth."* Our name, or our reputation, matters. As Christians, we carry with us the name that is above all names, the name of Jesus. When our name come up in conversation, a mental image of how others see us instantly emerges in their minds. Therefore, all confessing Christians should ask of themselves, "Is my walk aligned with my talk? Is my tongue captive to God's Word, or is it a captive servant of my flesh? Do others see Jesus in me? Is Jesus truly my Lord?" The answer to each question reveals much about our true identity, especially Whose we are.

Third: James will reveal our level of **Christian maturity**. Mature Christians are not on the mountain top one day and in the valley the next. A mature Christian is not controlled by a carnal mind nor easily moved and manipulated by circumstances. Mature Christians are single-minded in faith, speech, and actions. They are always bearing good fruit for the sake of the Kingdom. While none of us has arrived, we should be in a continual mode of growing into greater Christian maturity.

As we read and probe into the spiritual truths that James presents to the Church, he may come across as a hardnosed pastor who enjoys stomping on toes. The reality is that he loves us too much not to address the issues of life that all Christians face. As we enjoy this study together, we may need to continually remind ourselves that "God is speaking to me." Too often, we fail to receive God's message for ourselves because we want someone else to change. James is not speaking to someone else, dear reader. He is speaking to you.

THE AUTHOR OF THE
EPISTLE OF JAMES

Who was the author of the Book of James? Let me say from the outset that I do not believe there is a definitive answer to this question. There are at least three different men in Scripture with the name of James, two of whom were disciples of Jesus. Some make a valid point that James was a common Jewish name, so it is possible that there could have been hundreds more who could have penned this epistle. It is possible, but that theory is inconsistent with God's method of choosing known men in Scripture to be used as His authors.

1 – James, the son of Zebedee: This James was a brother to John, the beloved of Jesus, who was martyred a few years after the death and resurrection of Jesus. He, along with John and Peter, was chosen to accompany Jesus to the mountain where Jesus was transfigured. He was also chosen to accompany Jesus to the home of Jairus, whose daughter Jesus raised from the dead. Most importantly, he was chosen to accompany Jesus as a prayer intercessor in the Garden of Gethsemane as our Lord sought His Father's will concerning the Cross. James witnessed the ascension of Jesus into heaven following His resurrection and immediately began proclaiming the gospel of Jesus unto salvation. King Herod had him jailed and then beheaded in an effort to stop the Christian movement, which pleased the Pharisees. His martyrdom at the hands of Herod is believed to have taken place around 44 AD, and most theologians believe the Epistle of James was written after this date. Almost no one supports this most trusted disciple as authoring the Epistle of James to the Church.

2 – James the Less: James the Less was also one of the twelve disciples chosen by Jesus during His earthly ministry. He was probably called "the Less" due to his physical stature. Most assuredly, it was not because he was seen as less important. History says that he was martyred in 62 AD when persecutors of the Faith threw him from the pinnacle of the temple and then stoned and beat him to death as he prayed for them. Interestingly, Satan tempted Jesus to throw Himself from the pinnacle of the temple but was unsuccessful. Even though the time frame that would have allowed him to write this book coincides with the dates most historians and theologians believe James was penned, there simply is not enough known about James the Less in Scripture that would point to him as the author of this New Testament Book.

3 – James the Just, a son of Mary and a half-brother of Jesus. It is said that he was surnamed "the Just" by Hegesippus, a historian. This James was the half-brother of Jesus and brother of Jude. If I were pressed to pick the James that penned this letter, it would be this James. It was not until Jesus' resurrection and appearance to His half-brother that James believed on Jesus as the Messiah (1 Corinthians 15:7). The Apostle Paul mentions seeing "James, the Lord's brother," when he went up to Jerusalem in search of Peter. Paul went up again to Jerusalem fourteen years later and once again names this James in the context of being a pillar in the Church (Galatians 1:19, 2:9). Later, we see James asserting himself as a Church leader as recorded in Acts 15:13. Considerable debate and dissension had arisen among the brethren concerning Gentiles being received into the Church, and James rose to the occasion, offering solid leadership and counsel. With the preponderance of information made available, it would appear that James, the half-brother of Jesus and an esteemed Church leader, is the most logical to receive credit for writing the Epistle of James. You make the call.

Finally, we know that regardless of which James actually penned this letter of encouragement and instruction, it was inspired entirely by the person of the Holy Spirit. Taken in context, it is not the writer who actually wrote this epistle that should be of primary interest but the actual author, Jesus Christ, whom we seek as we carefully study His Word. Many pastors have sounded the warning of "getting our feet stomped on" when preaching from James, but that is not the case. It is indeed a book that warns of deception and the misuse of grace, but it is also the call of a loving pastor to trust in Jesus and Jesus alone.

SOME HELPFUL HINTS TO A SUCCESSFUL STUDY OF THE BOOK OF JAMES

1 – Read the letter in its entirety before you begin your study. Underline points of interest.

2 – Pray and ask God for wisdom and revelation of His Word.

3 – Don't focus on others when various situations are presented, but focus on how you see yourself.

4 – Accept as fact: You cannot change anyone else, but you can allow the Holy Spirit to change you.

5 – Remember that James did not write in chapter and verse. This was done by Bible scholars in an effort to help compartmentalize different thoughts and subjects, as well as creating a reference guide for finding particular verses. That said, it would be impossible to compartmentalize any part of James' instruction and teaching, as each verse builds and sustains both previous and latter truths.

PURPOSE

This commentary was written at the request of my most precious wife Penny, my daughter Casey, and most importantly, by the prompting of the Holy Spirit. It is my hope and prayer that all of my children, grandchildren, friends, and other readers will find this teaching commentary helpful in gleaning God's truths that are instrumental for living a victorious Christian life.

The *New American Standard Bible (NASB)* was used for this study because it is one of the most dependable of all Bible translations, having its origin in the most original Jewish scrolls. Bibles used for study purposes should always be carefully examined for their integrity, as some user-friendly Bibles are actually commentaries of current translations. That is not to suggest that these Bibles should never be used. They have a purpose and a place, especially in aiding new converts to understand Bible truths and events.

Hopefully, this commentary will be a blessing to all who read it and our Lord Jesus will be exalted. Keep in mind that this is a commentary, not a substitute for allowing God to speak individually to each and every reader.

I dedicate this book, *Practical Wisdom to Reign in Life*, to my best friend and the love of my life, my wife Penny. The year is 2019.

—Don Griffin

JAMES CHAPTER ONE

Vs. 1: *¹James, a bond-servant of God and of the Lord Jesus Christ, to the twelve tribes who are dispersed abroad: Greetings.*

If the writer of this letter is the half-brother of Jesus, he does not take this opportunity to exalt himself by calling attention to their family relationship. Instead, the writer declares himself to be a "bond-servant" of Jesus. He also chooses to exalt Jesus as the Son of God, declaring Him to be the Second Person of the Holy Trinity. As we begin our exciting journey through the Book of James, it is worth noting that the first eight verses provide valuable insight that will help us gain a foundational understanding of the entire epistle.

James was not the only writer to call himself a bond-servant of Christ Jesus. The apostle Paul called himself a bond-servant, as did Peter, John, and Jude. Mary, the mother of Jesus, called herself the bond-servant of the Lord when the angel Gabriel appeared to her. The term "bond-servant" is not a modern expression, but the nation of Israel that existed during the ministry of Jesus knew the expression quite well. In the Book of Exodus, chapter twenty-one, the term "bond-servant" is described in detail. Under Jewish Law, a person could become a slave or servant to a fellow Israelite if they failed to meet a monetary debt. After six-years of service, the debt was considered paid and they were free to leave. Of course, they were free to leave earlier if the debt was paid, but that seldom happened.

On occasion, there were servants who did not want to leave their master's house. If a servant served their master for six years and chose not to go free, they would declare publicly, "I love my master. I will not go out as a free man." Their master would then pierce their ear and place a ring in it. This signified to everyone that this person had chosen to become a life-long bond-servant. James is not using the term "bond-servant" lightly, and neither should we.

The Greek word for *greetings* is "Chairo," meaning "to be glad, or Godspeed, or rejoice." James had a great concern for the twelve tribes of Israel and for good reason. Israel, with small exception, had rejected Jesus as their Messiah. Today, as in that day, many Israelis around the world still consider Jesus to be a great prophet but not the Messiah. Israel was looking for a conquering Messiah who would free them from Rome and set up His Kingdom here on earth, but the meek and humble Jesus arrived in Jerusalem riding on a donkey. When He comes again, He will be riding a majestic white stallion, and the armies of heaven will be with Him. He will enter through the Eastern Gate of the city of Jerusalem and, with the breath of His mouth, slay His adversaries. With Satan in irons and sin held in bondage, Jesus will then rule and reign over all the earth for one thousand years. Can you say, Hallelujah?

One may well ask why this letter was written only to the twelve tribes when God had opened the door of His Church to Gentiles through the apostle Peter. God had shown up with great pomp and circumstance at the house of Cornelius, a Gentile, and saved the entire house. Not only were they saved, but they were filled to overflow with the Holy Spirit. So, the question could be posed, "Was James prejudiced?" No, James was not prejudiced, but many believing Jews were, and God did not want them to reject this powerful letter because he had included the Gentiles in his salutation.

There is an important lesson to be learned here. The lesson is to be obedient and fulfill the purpose and plan that God has for each of us. Had God impressed on James to include Gentiles in his salutation, he would have. Two thousand years later, the number of Gentiles who study and glean from this wonderful and insightful letter far outnumber those who are Jewish. In spite of severe persecution from both Romans and Jews, the key word from James to the Church is, "**Rejoice!**"

Vs. 2-4: *² Consider it all joy, my brethren, when you encounter various trials, ³ knowing that the testing of your faith produces endurance. ⁴ And let endurance have its perfect result, so that you may be perfect and complete, lacking in nothing.*

Jesus said, *"In the world you have tribulation"* (John 16:33), and as any serious student of life will attest, no truer words were ever spoken. Jesus never erred in word or deed, and He was exact when He warned about trials and tribulations. They are a part of life, and they will continue to be a part of life until Christ returns. Jesus was not exempt, the disciples were not exempt, and the early Church was not exempt. Some preach that because we live under a better covenant, we can shield ourselves from persecution if we have enough faith. Not so! After the Cross, the disciples were filled with faith after seeing the Lord raised from the dead, but their faith did not save them from suffering severe persecution. With the exception of John, all of the disciples were martyred for preaching the gospel of Jesus Christ.

Even so, there is good news to be proclaimed: No matter the severity of our trials or circumstances, God always supplies us with more than enough grace to traverse the storms of life. Amazingly, the more Christians are persecuted, the more the Church increases.

Having made that statement, we would be wise to hit the pause button and attempt to bring greater clarification to the question, "Why do bad things happen to good people? Is it God's way of teaching us something, or is it Satan's attempt to destroy us?" Please allow me to suggest three things that create trials and tribulations in the lives of us all. You may have more.

#1 – We live in a fallen world, and when people fall (literally or figuratively), they get hurt. Our physical bodies get hurt because the Law of Gravity always works. Our emotional minds get hurt by unkind words, deeds, and other disappointments of life. Anything that is negative or unpleasant gives our souls an opportunity to be in unrest, but it is in times of conflict that we discover a lot about ourselves. We may find that our faith was greater than we had ever imagined, or we may discover the exact opposite. Either way, our Christian maturity will be on display for all to see.

#2 – Satan is for now the prince and power of the air (Eph. 2:2). He will remain the ruler of the air until Christ returns, but every Christian needs to be aware that Jesus stripped him of his power over the Elect (saved). His premier weapon is to lure those who are not grounded in the Word into his traps of deception. Until Christ returns and locks him away, trials and tribulations will continue here on earth.

#3 – We suffer many trials in life because we, at times, make bad choices. Bad choices are usually those we make when we fail to seek the counsel of the Holy Spirit. We can take it to the bank, bad choices produce bad fruit, and no one enjoys eating bad fruit. James will also teach us that bad choices are a result of choosing the wisdom of the world instead of the wisdom of God. He will clearly reveal that there are indeed two types of wisdom. One is worldly (bad choices), and the other is from above, or Godly wisdom (good choices).

So why does God allow His Church to endure the unpleasantness of trials and tribulations? James tells us. His first purpose is to test our faith. Dear reader, you may struggle with this, but faith is the currency of heaven. Hebrews 11:6, *"And without faith it is impossible to please [God]."* How do we know that we have genuine faith? We cannot know unless our faith has been tested. But this we do know, "A faith untested is a faith that cannot be trusted." We can tell others of our great faith, but without a testimony to back it up, our words ring hollow. It is when the wind is howling and huge waves are crashing into our little boat that our faith is truly tested.

Allow me to share a quick testimony of a Christian wife and mother whose faith was severely tested.

My son received a call from a close friend informing him that his father-in-law had suffered a severe heart attack. It was his second heart attack, and it did not appear that he would live.

Upon hearing the news, my son and I drove immediately to the nearby hospital. We entered his room not knowing what we would encounter. Although he was gravely ill, he was awake and coherent. He said to us in a weak voice, "Mr. Don, this is what happens when you get too much stress." I responded, "We are here to pray for you. Let's believe that God will raise you up."

After praying a prayer of faith, I turned my attention to his wife and daughter. "I have prayed a prayer of faith. Now we must stand in faith and believe that God will raise him up. Do not under any circumstances speak any negative words that are contrary to our prayer."

Later that day, he was transferred to a hospital that was better equipped to handle his illness, but still, the prognosis remained grim. Soon after their arrival, a doctor came out and tried to prepare his wife for the worst. She replied, "Thank you for your report, but he is going to be fine." Shortly thereafter, a second doctor came out to prepare her for the inevitable. Her response was, "Thank you, but he is going to be fine." Exasperated, they sent a nurse to convey the severity of his condition. The nurse expounded in vivid detail the many reasons that she needed to face reality, but she again responded, "He is going to make it. He will be okay." Her faith prevailed!

A few days later, he walked out of the hospital. In less than two weeks he was back at work. That is faith. The storm raged, but she refused to receive the bad reports.

"Death and life are in the power of the tongue" (Prov. 18:21) is foreign to most of the Christian Church, and that needs to change. God's Word is Truth. Truth plus faith will always triumph over facts. We will look at this important subject in greater depth in Chapter Three.

James tells us that God allows our faith to be tested because it will produce endurance. Time has a way of teaching us that life is not a sprint, it is a race of endurance. Endurance keeps marriages together, businesses alive, and hope in our hearts. Endurance will stop us from searching for a back door when times are tough and running away looks good. Endurance is never the result of pleasantries.

No, just the opposite. Growing up, my father told me about life during the Great Depression. He told of the months he worked on the railroad for fifty cents a day, of the many times my mother stood in long lines to get a block of government cheese. They did not know where the next meal was coming from, or even if there would be one. The only thing that sustained them was their faith in God. That was endurance.

James goes on to reveal that endurance will bring about a perfect result, so that we will be perfect and complete, lacking nothing. Make no mistake about it, God places every born-again believer on His potter's wheel for His purpose. His purpose is to shape us into vessels for His use, to remove the cracks, scars, and blemishes that were placed there by sin and the disappointments of life. At times, His wheel may prove to be painful, but when He has had His way, out comes a vessel that is worthy of the Master (see Isaiah 64:8). When we go into a store looking for a piece of pottery, it is not the ones that are cracked and full of blemishes that we desire. It is the ones that were perfected on the potter's wheel. In the same way, the world is not enamored with Christians who live or talk differently than they, but they are attracted to those who exemplify Jesus.

It is important to understand that in the Spirit realm, the spirit of every born-again Christian was made complete the moment we accepted Jesus as Savior (Col. 2:9, 2 Cor. 5:17). To that, we can shout, "Hallelujah!" But God was not finished. He not only breathed life into our spirit, but He also saved our soul and sealed us with His Holy Spirit (1 Pet. 1:9, Eph. 1:13).

Caution! Even though those wonderful, irrevocable events took place, our flesh, which includes the mind, will, and emotions, did not get saved. That is why so many Christians stay confused. They ask themselves, "If I am saved, why do I still sin and act so ungodly at times?" The answer is simply that our minds (flesh) were not saved. Our natural mind (will and emotions) cannot be born again. "That which is born of flesh is flesh, and that which is born of Spirit is spirit" (John 3:6). The apostle Paul warned, *"Do not be conformed to this world, but transformed by the renewing of your mind"* (Rom. 12:2). God's Word, and only God's Word, has the power to renew our mind to spiritual truth.

Vs. 5-8: *⁵ But if any of you lacks wisdom, let him ask of God, who gives to all generously and without reproach, and it will be given to him. ⁶ But he must ask in faith without any doubting, for the one who doubts is like the surf of the sea, driven and tossed by the wind. ⁷ For that man ought not to expect that he will receive anything from the Lord, ⁸ being a double-minded man, unstable in all his ways.*

I wrote earlier that the first eight verses set the theme for the entire letter, and they do. They are the foundation on which James builds his message to the Church. He greatly desires that we see our loving Father as the abundant Provision for every area of life, so that we are not lured into the world's system. As James continually reveals truths that are intended to steer us from the deception of being double-minded, he will continually warn of the danger of walking with one foot in the Kingdom and one foot in the world. That is what double-minded Christians unwittingly do. They profess God as King but have no more faith than their lost neighbor.

So how do we become Kingdom-minded and full of God's wisdom? Remember that every question we have about Scripture is always an open-book test, so James tells us, "If any of you lacks wisdom, let him ask God." Please allow me to share a simple truth relative to God's Word: Knowledge (Scripture) + Understanding (revelation) = Wisdom.

Isaiah the prophet declared, "God's thoughts are not our thoughts, neither are our ways His ways" (Is. 55:8). One thing is for certain. God is God, and we are not. There are thoughts that belong to God that are greater than our finite brains can comprehend, but there are many thoughts that He longs for us to know.

Jesus came to earth to save a lost and dying world, but He also came that we might see the Father. The Father's thoughts toward us are gushing with unconditional love, a love so great that His only begotten Son, in obedience to His Father, suffered the agony of thirty-nine lashes with a Roman whip and crucifixion on a cross. He could have called legions of angels, but He refused to take a way of escape, allowing Himself to become the human sacrifice for the sins of all mankind (Matt. 26:53).

When we read or study in the Old Testament, we should thoughtfully consider that most prophecies were types and shadows of the coming Messiah, the Cross, and the New Covenant of Grace. Millions of people around the world are still making the same request asked by Phillip the disciple, "Lord, show us the Father, and it is enough for us." Jesus replied to him, "He who has seen Me has seen the Father" (John 14:8-9).

Will we know it all? No, not on this side of heaven. We will never attain to the fullness of God in thought, word, or deed while we live here on earth. What we can attain to is the destiny that God planned for us before we were even born. As an old saint of God used to say, "Brothers and sisters, if we aren't moving forward in our daily walk, we are backsliding."

Let me attest that for more than fifty years, the Lord has allowed me to teach His Holy Word. I certainly did not know everything when I began, and I am a long way from knowing everything today. I readily admit that there are some Scriptures that I teach differently today than I did in the past. I had a zeal for God's Word, but, as Paul wrote in Romans 10:2, *"not in accordance with knowledge."* Thankfully, all of God's gifts are irrevocable, and that is inclusive of teaching. Instead of sitting me on the bench, our Father continued to give me an increase of His wisdom, something I have continued to pray for. He will do the same for anyone who hungers and thirsts after Him, and that, dear reader, is inclusive of you.

Have I arrived? No, I have not arrived. None of us will arrive until we see our Jesus face to face. The apostle Paul concluded in 1 Corinthians 13:12, *"For now we see in a mirror dimly, but then face to face, now I know in part, but then I will know fully just as I also have been fully known."* To know and understand all Scripture is not the question we should ask. What are we doing with what He has already given us is the question. The same spirit that lived in Paul now lives and resides in us. Listen to the words of Paul the preacher, *"And my message and my peaching were not in persuasive words of* [worldly] *wisdom, but in demonstration of the Spirit and of power, so that your faith would not rest on the wisdom of men, but on the power of God"* (1 Cor. 2:4-5 bracketed words added).

Paul did not wait until he knew everything to preach the gospel, and neither should we. Neither preaching nor teaching may be our spiritual gift, but we all have a spiritual gift, and we all have a ministry that needs to be used in the body of Christ. God will not give us more until we step out in faith and begin using what we already have.

Concerning wisdom, King Solomon, a man of extraordinary wisdom, penned this warning in Proverbs 14:12, *"There is a way which seems right to a man, but its end is the way of death."* We must be certain that we do not allow the wisdom of the world to contaminate the wisdom of God. Is that possible? No, God's wisdom cannot be contaminated, but our minds can become contaminated if we allow ourselves to become double-minded. The wisdom of the world always paints a rosy picture, but the picture painted never tells the entire story. It does not reveal the potholes and raging rivers that cannot be crossed because the bridges are gone. It never shows the hurt, the worry, or the strife concealed in broken hearts, and it never shows the unwary that the road they are traveling will lead to a dead end. Mark it down, worldly wisdom always leads to a dead-end road.

James gives us the antidote to the world's wisdom. He instructs us to ask for godly wisdom, but he also reminds us that we must ask "in faith." Faith is the key that unlocks the riches (our inheritance) of God's Kingdom. If we are truthful with ourselves, we will have to admit that there are times when our circumstances seem greater than our faith. We want to believe, and we want to have faith, but like the man who asked Jesus to cast a demon out of his son, we may say, "Lord, help my unbelief" (Mark 9:24).

Perhaps you are one of many who think they missed out when it comes to faith. Take heart. You do have faith. Romans 12:3, *"God has allotted to each a measure of faith."* Meditate on this powerful truth: God always supplies the provision before our need arrives. Everything Adam and Eve needed was created before God placed them in the Garden. It is the same with salvation. He placed inside each of us an intuitive knowledge of the Creator while we were still lost. That knowledge reveals to every sinner that there is a God Who desires to be our Savior (Romans 1:19-20). We were not seeking God, but He was relentlessly seeking after us with an offer of forgiveness and immaculate Grace.

Ephesians 2:8, "For by grace you have been saved through faith." It is important to understand that we were not saved by grace alone, nor were we saved by faith alone. We were saved by placing our faith in God's abundant offer of grace. Having received this great salvation, our faith will remain in infancy unless we choose to renew our minds with the knowledge of His Word. One well-known pastor once said, "We have more babies in the sanctuary than we have in the nursery."

Here is another foundational truth: Our faith will never rise to a higher level than our ability to believe the promises given in God's Word. Not having faith in God and trusting Him to do what He has promised is the result of "unbelief." We must not be deceived. Unbelief is birthed when we trust in our five senses—sight, smell, taste, touch, and hearing—instead of the Word and promises of God. Unbelief is our constant nemesis, a nemesis that spreads doubt and fear through spoken words. Fear causes worry, worry creates anxiety, and anxiety opens the door to the tormentor, Satan. God does not want us to live lives laced with fear and worry. The remedy? "Trust in God" (Mark 11:22). How? A good way for us to begin is by spending time with Him. It is there that we can bare our souls to Him. As we learn to rest in Jesus, our fears of loss and punishment will fade away. Guaranteed!

We need to remind ourselves of the recurring chorus that saturates the whole of James' letter, the warning of being double-minded, of attempting to trust God while putting a greater faith in the world's system. God says that the double-minded man will not receive anything from Him.

Vs. 9-11: *⁹ But the brother of humble circumstances is to glory in his high position; ¹⁰ and the rich man is to glory in his humiliation, because like flowering grass he will pass away. ¹¹ For the sun rises with a scorching wind and withers the grass; and its flower falls off and the beauty of its appearance is destroyed; so too the rich man in the midst of his pursuits will fade away.*

Let's be careful with these verses and not be guilty of developing spiritual dyslexia. There is no virtue in being poor, and there is no virtue in being rich, so what is God saying? He is saying that Christian virtue and worth are not measured by the things we do or the things we own. In truth, our virtue and worth is not measured at all. It is simply that we are known by the fruit we produce with the full knowledge that God owns the vineyard. Proverbs 10:15, *"The rich man's wealth is his fortress, the ruin of the poor is their poverty."* This proverb expresses the mind-set of the unsaved who pursue wealth, but it also expresses the mindset of many Christians. James addresses these issues in verses nine and ten, making an appeal that each of us recognize who we are and whose we are in Christ.

Likewise, the rich man must remember that his riches are not his fortress. It was not his riches that saved him, but, rather, it was his faith in God's abundant grace. Having received salvation by humbling himself before God, he must continue to humble himself so that he is not drawn away by the lust of riches.

Vs. 12: *¹² Blessed is a man who perseveres under trial; for once he has been approved, he will receive the crown of life which the Lord has promised to those who love Him.*

This is a continuation of the previous verses. Everyone, the rich, the poor, and those in between, will encounter trials while here on earth. Going through trials and adversities are not pleasant for the moment, but it is in the trials of life that we are spiritually enriched. James is reminding us that our spiritual position guarantees that we will receive the crown of life. This glorious knowledge increases our faith and further equips us to successfully traverse through trials when they do come.

Vs. 13-15: *¹³ Let no one say when he is tempted, "I am being tempted by God," for God cannot be tempted by evil, and He Himself does not tempt anyone. ¹⁴ But each one is tempted when he is carried away and enticed by his own lust. ¹⁵ Then when lust has conceived, it gives birth to sin; and when sin is accomplished, it brings forth death.*

The rich point is now made that God never, under any circumstances, tempts anyone to sin. However, James reminds us that we are very capable of sinning if we allow our minds to yield to our enemy's enticements (lust comes in many forms). Once our minds are allowed to yield to carnality and temptation, sin will conceive. Conception allows the corruptible seed to give birth, and in due time, death will follow.

NOTE: The fact that we do not actually see death in the form of a body does not mean that death has not occurred. Spiritual death comes in many forms. Left unresolved, sin can cause death in our marriages, our children, and our bodies. Jesus paid the price for our sins, but that does not change the fact that there is always a consequence to sin. Yet, here is a question that begs to be answered, "When we do sin, why do we run away from our heavenly Father instead of running to Him?" There may be several reasons, but the greatest and foremost reason is due to shame. We are ashamed of our sin, and because we are ashamed, we are unwilling to enter into the presence of our Heavenly Father. Satan and his demons are well aware of the effects of shame, so they quickly bombard us with even more guilt. Dear readers, as long as we allow our enemy to keep us from the Father, we will continue to wallow in our shame. We must learn to come quickly to the Father, for the sinless One, Jesus, has paid our sin debt in full, past, present, and future.

There is a spiritual Truth in Ephesians 2:4-9 that many Christians are unaware of: *"But God, being rich in mercy, because of His great love with which He loved us, even when we were dead in our transgressions, made us alive together with Christ (by grace you have been saved), and raised us up with Him, and seated us with Him in the heavenly places in Christ Jesus, so that in the ages to come He might show the surpassing riches of His grace in kindness toward us in Christ Jesus. For by grace you have been saved through faith; and that not of yourselves, it is the gift of God; not as a result of works, so that no one may boast."* That means that everything named is not only under the feet of Jesus, but everything named is under our feet as well. Satan would have us believe that a certain sin or sins have a stronghold from which we cannot get free, but he is a liar. We are not trying to get free, for Jesus has already set us free! The only stronghold that can control us is in our mind, not our spirit. *"So if the Son makes you free, you will be free indeed"* (John 8:36).

Do you want some more good news? Under the New Covenant of Grace, God's children no longer experience spiritual death because of sin. How can that be, you ask? Because we have been washed in the blood of Jesus. Having washed us and removed our sin, Jesus is now our constant Advocate.

Jesus died once for sin for all time. Christ is not going back to the Cross because we at times allow ourselves to buy into the temptations of sin. *"We have been sanctified through the offering of the body of Jesus Christ once for all"* (Heb. 10:10). Satan has been dealt a death blow, but he runs around growling in an effort to keep us from knowing it. If all of this seems too good to be true, it is not. It is all true.

The apostle Paul was very cognizant of the fact that every time he preached the Gospel of Grace, this question would be asked, *"Are we to continue in sin so that grace may increase?"* (Rom. 6:1). How did Paul answer? He answered it in the same way we should answer, by responding, "May it never be!" (Rom. 6:2).

News flash! Satan can tempt us, but he cannot make us sin. So, why do we still sin? We sin because we at times allow our flesh to control our carnal minds instead of the indwelling Holy Spirit. We sin because there is pleasure in sin for a season (Heb. 11:25). Satan would have us believe that temptation is sin, but temptation is not sin. With every temptation, God has given us a way of escape. Even Jesus was tempted, but He never allowed the temptation to find a place in his heart. It is when we allow temptation to move from our head to our heart that we allow sin to be birthed. Once sin is birthed, nothing but the mercies of God can stop it from having its full effect. Sin always has a consequence.

Vs. 16-18: *¹⁶ Do not be deceived, my beloved brethren. ¹⁷ Every good thing given and every perfect gift is from above, coming down from the Father of lights, with whom there is no variation or shifting shadow. ¹⁸ In the exercise of His will He brought us forth by the word of truth, so that we would be a kind of first fruits among His creatures.*

The following will sound like a "Duh" statement, but I want to make the statement anyway. "The problem with a deceived person is that they are deceived." In other words, they believe that a lie is truth. James is fully aware of the wiles of the enemy, so he issues a warning concerning the deception of thinking wrong toward God.

In verses 17 and 18, James makes it abundantly clear that God does not send good things into our lives when He is having a good day, and bad things into our lives when He is irritated. He does not send good things when we are good and bad things when we are bad. The Church is easily confused about this because we are taught the very opposite when we are children. The world sings, "Here comes Santa Claus," and that is okay, but God is not Santa Claus. Neither is He checking our naughty list to see if we have been bad or good. God does not give or withhold blessings based on our behavior. James is trying to simplify this truth by saying, "All good things come from above!" It is religion that continues to complicate what God is doing. "It cannot be so simple," they say. "We must do something to earn His blessings."

That God is not sending bad things into our lives is not

to suggest that God does not correct us, because He does. Neither is this to suggest that we cannot glean and grow when sickness or adversity comes our way, because we can, and we should. However, let the point be made once again that God is not sending sickness and adversity into our lives as He did on occasion under the Old Covenant. Earthly priests were the mediators under the old covenant of Law, but today, our High Priest is Jesus Christ Himself.

The angel's message of *"peace on earth"* was to let us know that the war between God and man is over. When we accept Christ, we gain peace with God. God still corrects us, but not in the same ways that He, at times, corrected Israel when they refused Him and sought after other gods. Today, He corrects us with the voice of His Spirit, through pastors and teachers, through sermons, and through the testimonies of godly people whom He orchestrates to cross our paths. Most of the time, God corrects and teaches us by His Word (see 2 Timothy 3:16). If we fail to listen to His correction, we may soon discover that Satan has gained a spiritual entrance into our lives.

Jesus prayed to His Father (and ours), *"Thy will be done on earth as it is in heaven"* (see Matt. 6:10). There is no poverty, sickness, or disease in Heaven, and they are not His will for us here on earth. We are God's first fruits from the seed of His Son Jesus that should cause a lost and dying world to hunger for Him. Sickness, poverty, and disease are the corrupted fruits of Satan. They are not a part of God's plan for His children, but they are part of the curse that resulted from the sin of Adam.

Vs. 19-21: *¹⁹ This you know, my beloved brethren. But everyone must be quick to hear, slow to speak and slow to anger; ²⁰ for the anger of man does not achieve the righteousness of God. ¹²¹ Therefore, putting aside all filthiness and all that remains of wickedness, in humility receive the word implanted, which is able to save your souls.*

Let me ask a question: "Has there ever been as much hate and anger as is evidenced today?" I think not, and these evils will only increase as the end days draw ever closer. The world is saturated with anger and strife, but the world is not alone. Many Christians also deal with a spirit of anger. It could be argued, however, that there are two types of anger. Jesus was angry when He saw the Pharisee's hardness of heart concerning the man with the withered hand. They were appalled that Jesus would heal this man on the Sabbath Day, but heal him He did. It is not that kind of anger that James is talking about. He is talking about unrighteous anger, the kind most of us spew on others from time to time.

Proverbs 18:13 warns, *"He who gives an answer before he hears, it is folly and shame to him."* Most of the things we hear do not require deep thought or prayer before we answer because we know light from darkness. Yet, there are times and moments when we need to deliberate before we speak. Words are powerful. Words are seeds that empower life or death. They have the power to unify and satisfy, but they also have the power to bring about division and disagreement. Try as we may, we cannot justify angry words that are fueled by our flesh and emotions.

James calls this type of anger filthiness that comes as a result of wickedness. Once again, he offers us a choice. We can speak and act as the world acts, or we can follow the example of Jesus and speak words of love and forgiveness. The latter is able to keep our souls in peace.

Vs. 22-24: *^{22}But prove yourselves doers of the word, and not merely hearers who delude themselves. ^{23} For if anyone is a hearer of the word and not a doer, he is like a man who looks at his natural face in a mirror; ^{24} for once he has looked at himself and gone away, he has immediately forgotten what kind of person he was.*

James is challenging every Christian to remember that we are commanded to "Go," not "Sit," for we all are called to be "Ambassadors for Christ." *Webster* defines **ambassador** as, "the highest-ranking diplomat of one country to another." That is who we are. We are of the highest rank because the Holy Spirit of God lives in us, the hope of glory. We have what the world needs, a hope that leads to the salvation of our souls. Anyone who is without Christ is without hope. That is why millions of unsaved people are overdosing on drugs. They are looking for hope in the form of drugs, alcohol, and illicit sex.

James now follows with another analogy that is grossly misunderstood by many Christians. He tells us that if we look into a mirror and all that we see is the image of ourselves, then we have forgotten what Christ did for us spiritually. Thankfully, the reflection we see is only one third of who we really are. We cannot see them with our physical eyes, but there is a soul person living in our body as well as the Third Person of the Trinity. It is called 3D. We must daily remind ourselves that the reflection we see in a mirror is God's grandest accomplishment. We are God's masterpieces.

Vs. 25: *^{25}But one who looks intently at the perfect law, the law of liberty, and abides by it, not having become a forgetful hearer but an effectual doer, this man shall be blessed in what he does.*

The Cross changed everything. The Son of God cried out from the Cross, *"It is finished"* (John 19:30). Because of His finished work, every person born of woman has the offer of the forgiveness of their sins that leads to eternal salvation. Those words also brought an end to the Old Covenant and ushered in the New. No longer are we governed by the Old Covenant Law of Moses. The underlying theme of the Old Covenant was "Do." The overt theme of the New Covenant is "Done." Jesus did what no man before Him had ever done; He kept the Old Covenant Law to the letter. In doing so, He rendered the Old Covenant obsolete (see Heb. 9:15 AMP). He entered this world sinless, and He left this world the same way.

No pun intended, but we are not throwing stones when we say that most Christians who demand that we must continue to keep the Law of Moses have trouble quoting The Ten Commandments, much less the other six-hundred-plus laws that comprise the entirety of the Mosaic Law. Concerning the Old Covenant, Paul wrote, *"[R]ealizing the fact that law is not made for a righteous person, but for those who are lawless and rebellious, for the ungodly and sinners, for the unholy and profane"* (1 Tim. 1:9).

Thankfully, Jesus made us righteous and freed us from the Law that no one could keep, making us recipients of the New Covenant Law of Liberty. What is the Law of Liberty? Jesus said, *"You shall love the Lord your God with all of your heart, and with all your soul, and with all of your strength, and with all of your mind, and your neighbor as yourself"* (Luke 10:27). The Law of Liberty gives us the freedom to do anything that the Holy Spirit directs us to do, remembering that the foundation of our freedom is unconditional love. When we abide in the Law of Liberty, we effortlessly fulfill The Ten Commandments, and the others as well.

Vs. 26-27: *²⁶ If anyone thinks himself to be religious, and yet does not bridle his tongue but deceives his own heart, this man's religion is worthless. ²⁷ Pure and undefiled religion in the sight of our God and Father is this: to visit orphans and widows in their distress, and to keep oneself unstained by the world.*

As we continue our study, it will become evident that James takes his position as Church leader very seriously. Over and again, he warns about the deception and lies of the enemy. Here, he explains that mature Christianity is closely tied to our relationship with Jesus. When our relationship with our Lord is flourishing, it is not nearly as difficult to control our tongues, our words, and our actions. When we are not in a right relationship, our words and actions will expose us.

Our spiritual heart is the final part of our soul realm (heart, mind, and soul), having faithfully recorded everything that has occurred in our lives since birth. Proverbs 4:23, *"Watch over your heart with all diligence, for from it flow the springs of life."* Satan's intent is to program our hearts with deceit and lies, a deceit that many Christians have bought in to. How do we avoid Satan's entrapment? We do so by programming our hearts and minds with the Word of God. Jesus said, *"I chose you out of the world, therefore the world hates you"* (John 15:19). In John 17:16, He makes it clear that our citizenship is not here on earth. We are in the world, but not of the world. The real truth is that we are Pilgrims passing through, but God does not intend for us to pass through without making a difference. While we are here, we should joyfully strive to be a beacon, a light that shines in darkness.

We have all heard some well-meaning person say, "Don't put your tent stakes too deep because your citizenship is in heaven." It sounds spiritual, but what does the Bible say? *"Enlarge the place of your tent; stretch out the curtains of your dwellings, spare not; lengthen your cords and strengthen your pegs"* (Is. 54:2). We are temporary citizens of earth, but God wants us to make a difference for His Kingdom while we are here. We need to meet each day with a smile on our face, a purpose in our steps, and a determination to make a difference in someone's life. We must daily remind ourselves that because we are in Christ, we are victors, not victims.

As we come to the close of Chapter One, James makes a very simple declaration that divides the "religious" from the "bond-servant." He reminds us that helping orphans and widows is doing the true work of Jesus. Orphans and widows are not able to repay us, but God is keeping records, and one day He Himself will repay us.

The following statement may come as a shock, but here it is. Hunger, especially among school-aged children, still exists here in America, one of the richest countries on earth. Researchers have found that a significant percentage of school-aged children, at least one in six, will eat their last meal at school on Friday and will not eat again until they return to school on Monday morning. Chances are great that the same conditions exist in areas near you. What a joy it is to be a small part of a ministry that takes food baskets to entire families. There is a reason that James declared, "Be a doer of the Word."

JAMES
CHAPTER TWO

Vs. 1-4: *¹My brethren, do not hold your faith in our glorious Lord Jesus Christ with an attitude of personal favoritism. ²For if a man comes into your assembly with a gold ring and dressed in fine clothes, and there also comes in a poor man in dirty clothes, ³and you pay special attention to the one who is wearing the fine clothes, and say, "You sit here in a good place," and you say to the poor man, "You stand over there, or sit down by my footstool," ⁴have you not made distinctions among yourselves, and become judges with evil motives?*

We will not hear a message preached very often on personal favoritism, but then, we will not hear a message preached on several of the issues that James is more than willing to address. In these verses, James is exposing a sin problem that existed in the early church and continues to surface two thousand years later, that of personal favoritism for personal gain. It is a challenge that each of us needs to address in our own heart. We have all witnessed the hand of personal favoritism shown to those of position and social status, and we have all witnessed the rejection of people because they lacked position and status.

Allow me to share an example that helps make this point. I was in attendance at a particular church that was enjoying a fifth Sunday dinner on the grounds. Long tables were filled with all types of delicious food, more than an abundance for the number of people present. In attendance were some children from a rather poor neighborhood. They had been attending Sunday School for a few weeks, but they always came alone, not with their parents. It was easy to discern from their dress and behavior that their situation was less than advantageous.

Upon seeing the abundance on the tables, the excitement and anticipation of enjoying the voluminous array of food was evident. They eagerly filled plates for themselves and then began the task of filling plates to take home. As they filled their take-home plates, a member of the church began to scold them for their actions. Upset and embarrassed, off they went with- out their plates, and to my recollection, they never returned. The oldest of those children is now an adult who, for business purposes, comes into my office on occasion. Sadly, her face is always a picture of despair and pain. Was that day a turning point in her life? I cannot answer that question, and in all likelihood, there were many other negative issues that she had to deal with as a child. Still, this church missed an excellent opportunity to present

Jesus to those children. Would the same attitude have prevailed if they had been children from a prominent family? What do you think? That is exactly the reason James addresses the subject of favoritism.

James, never a fence sitter, was not pleased when members of the church showed preference to those of means and avoided those less fortunate. He was reminding everyone that Jesus died for all, both the rich and the poor, the godly and the ungodly. Romans 2:11 declares, *"There is no partiality with God."* Both the rich and the poor are saved because they repent of their sins and place their faith in the shed blood of Jesus, nothing more and nothing less. James calls a spade a spade by identifying attitudes of favoritism as "evil."

Vs. 5-10: *⁵ Listen, my beloved brethren: did not God choose the poor of this world to be rich in faith and heirs of the kingdom which He promised to those who love Him? ⁶ But you have dishonored the poor man. Is it not the rich who oppress you and personally drag you into court? ⁷ Do they not blaspheme the fair name by which you have been called? ⁸ If, however, you are fulfilling the royal law according to the Scripture, "You shall love your neighbor as yourself," you are doing well. ⁹ But if you show partiality, you are committing sin and are convicted by the law as transgressors. ¹⁰ For whoever keeps the whole law and yet stumbles in one point, he has become guilty of all.*

Israel had been indoctrinated by the ruling class, most notably the Pharisees, to believe that riches were the result of God's favor, while misfortune and poverty were the result of God's judgment. That is why the disciples were amazed when Jesus said of the rich young ruler, *"How hard it is for those who trust in riches to enter the kingdom of God!"* (Mark 10:24 NKJV). James was not prejudiced against those who were rich, but he did not want those of the Faith to fawn over people of status and wealth.

Jesus did not die for some. He died for all! Titus 2:11 makes this wonderful declaration, "For the grace of God has appeared, bringing salvation to all men." The word "grace" can always be interchanged with the name "Jesus," for Jesus appeared, bringing salvation to all men. Prior to His coming, Israel looked to the Laws of Moses and the Passover as their avenue to God. They understood that the Passover Feast and the sacrifice given was an atonement for their sins, but with small exception, they misunderstood the real purpose of the Law.

The Law was much more than The Ten Commandments that most of Christianity is familiar with. In fact, there were six hundred and eleven laws that covered three different parts of society. There were civil laws, moral laws, and there were ceremonial laws. All of these laws combined did not have the power to save one lost soul. That is not to demean or diminish the Law, for God had a purpose in giving the Law to the nation of Israel. The purpose was to expose the sin nature that every unsaved person is born with and drive them to the Savior.

Unfortunately, many Christians still live their lives under the Law that the apostle Paul called, *"The ministry of death, in letters engraved on stone"* (2 Cor. 3:7). Why the confusion? It is hard to define as there are several reasons, but the main culprit may be many of the messages we hear preached. Many well-meaning pastors are still sending a mixed message of Law and Grace to their congregations. Jesus said, *"No one puts new wine into old wineskins; otherwise the wine will burst the skins, and the wine is lost and the skins as well"* (Mark 2:22). Jesus was reminding us that the Old Covenant of Law is not to be mixed with the New Covenant of Grace. However, Jesus made it clear, He did not come to abolish the Law, He came to fulfill the Law, and so He did (Matt. 5:17).

Jesus kept the Laws of Moses perfectly, but no other person born of woman can say the same. *"For all have sinned and fall short of the glory of God"* (Rom. 3:23). As long as there are lost people in need of the Savior, there will remain a need for the Law. Paul wrote to a young preacher named Timothy, *"Law is not made for a righteous person, but for those who are lawless"* (1 Tim. 1:9).

Try as we may, we cannot change ourselves from the outside in. Many have tried, but all have failed. Those who insist on trying to change themselves to please God by their works will live lives of frustration and disappointment. Only the Holy Spirit has the life-changing power to change the heart of man, and He does so from the inside out. For most of us, the change is gradual, but we can take solace in Paul's declaration: *"For I am confident of this very thing, that He who began a good work in you will perfect it until the day of Christ Jesus"* (Phil. 1:6). James did not want the Bride of Christ, the Church, to lose sight of the fact that the Cross is proof positive that Jesus loves everyone the same, no exceptions.

Vs. 11-13: *__11__ For He who said, "Do not commit adultery," also said, "Do not commit murder." Now if you do not commit adultery, but do commit murder, you have become a transgressor of the law. __12__ So speak and so act as those who are to be judged by the law of liberty. __13__ For judgment will be merciless to one who has shown no mercy; mercy triumphs over judgment.*

In Christian circles, the most profound sermon preached by Jesus is referred to as, "The Sermon on the Mount." The Bible says that the multitudes were amazed at His teaching. Why were they amazed at His teaching? The Bible tells us that it was because *"He was teaching them as one having authority"* (Matt. 7:29). All of us have listened to preachers and teachers who gave out a lot of information, but their messages were as boring as watching the grass grow. Thankfully, the reverse is also true. We have all heard preachers and teachers that we could listen to for hours. What is the difference? It is all about the anointing, and Jesus walked in the anointing. As he preached to the multitude, He intentionally raised the bar of righteousness to an entirely different level, a level so high that it completely imploded the religious Laws that ruled over the Old Covenant.

Jesus addressed the issue of murder by saying, *"You have heard that the ancients were told, 'You shall not commit murder' and 'Whoever commits murder shall be liable to the court.' But I say to you that everyone who is angry with his brother shall be guilty before the court; and whoever says to his brother, 'You good-for-nothing,' shall be guilty before the supreme court"* (Matt. 5:21-22). Wow! Are you serious?

And if that were not enough, He then cuts to the core, *"You have heard that it was said, 'You shall not commit adultery'; but I say to you that everyone who looks at a woman with lust for her has already committed adultery with her in his heart"* (Matt. 5:27-28).

Get the picture? Jesus went past the outward man and bored directly into the spiritual heart of man. Sin was exposed for what it really is, a leprosy so insidious that no amount of works can remove it. The picture became clearer, but many were not willing to receive it. What a revelation! Sin is more than an act of commission, it is the essence of the thoughts and words that emanate from our heart.

When I was growing up, my parents attended an old country church whose small congregation consisted of bona fide God-loving Christians. It also consisted of preachers whose understanding of Grace was very limited, so they preached with great tenacity what they had been taught, the Law of Moses, of do's and don'ts. This is certainly not meant to be an indictment of those men of God because they had every good intention. In my case, the Law did exactly what it was supposed to do, it drove me into the arms of Jesus.

Someone said, "It is better to be scared into heaven than to be lulled into hell," and there is surely some measure of truth in that statement. Yet, here is the point. The Law drove me to the Savior, but because I never heard the gospel of Grace preached when I was younger, I lived for years trying to please God with my works. Try as I might, I felt that I could never do enough to please the Lord, so I found myself running away from Him instead of to Him. I believed in my heart that God was not only measuring my sins, but that He was not pleased with me because I still sinned.

Thankfully, Romans 8:1 refutes such wayward theology. It boldly proclaims, *"Therefore* [referring to the finished work of Jesus] *there is now no condemnation for those who are in Christ Jesus."* The Holy Spirit is our very Best Friend, and His will is to help us do the will of our Father. He is continually whispering into our spiritual ears, offering direction, purpose, and power. He will convict us when we sin, but He never condemns us. Instead of condemnation, He is constantly reminding us that we are new creations, that the old man has passed away and all things have become new. If we suffer from condemnation, it is not from God.

Some cry out to God for justice. Not me. I want no part of justice. I want mercy. What do the Scriptures say? *"For all have sinned and fall short of the glory of God"* (Rom. 3:23). Since we ourselves desire for God to show us mercy and extend His marvelous grace, should we not be willing to extend mercy and grace to others, and to those who have offended us, to those who have not lived up to the standard we set for them? The apostle Paul wrote to the church in Galatia, many of whom were beginning to embrace the false teaching that the mercies and grace of Jesus were not enough, *"You foolish Galatians, who has bewitched you?"* (Gal. 3:1).

Knowing who we are and whose we are is huge. God is not trying to break the bondages and addictions that have prevailed over man since the fall of Adam. He already has. Jesus said, *"You will know the Truth, and the Truth will set you free"* (John 8:32). Our works cannot set us free, The Ten Commandments cannot set us free, and no book written on success can set us free. We are free because of the finished work of Jesus.

Meditate now on this truth:

**It is no longer what we do
that allows us into the presence of God.
It is all about what Jesus has done.**

Vs. 14-17: *¹⁴ What use is it, my brethren, if someone says he has faith but he has no works? Can that faith save him? ¹⁵ If a brother or sister is without clothing and in need of daily food, ¹⁶ and one of you says to them, "Go in peace, be warmed and be filled," and yet you do not give them what is necessary for their body, what use is that? ¹⁷ Even so faith, if it has no works, is dead, being by itself.*

James is asking several heart-to-heart questions in these verses, questions that all of us need to address in our own lives. As we attempt to answer these questions, it would be wise to also look at what James is not saying. He is not saying that works can save us. Neither is he saying that works can keep us saved. What he is saying is that we who are of the Faith need to put our faith to work, always being mindful of the needy and those who need help.

Recently, my wife and I were returning home from a short trip, so we pulled into a gas station to refuel. As I was putting fuel in my car, I noticed a well-dressed African-American man standing close by. I spoke and asked the usual, "How are you doing," and he responded, "Not very good." He went on to tell me that he was trying to get home, but he was out of money and out of gas. In obvious despair, he cried out, "I've been here for hours; no one will help me." I am sure that most of us have been in similar situations, so we ask ourselves, "Is this guy real, or is he a sham?" But there was something about him. He was not the normal sham guy. He was real, and I could see myself standing where he was. After a quick prayer for confirmation, I went to his car, placed my card into the meter, and told him to fill up. As I walked back toward my car he ran to me and said, "Mister, can I give you a hug?"

The next morning while teaching Sunday School, the Lord spoke clearly and led me to share the incident with the class. It was not to tell them what a great guy I was and how generous I had been. No, just the opposite. As I drove away from that gas station that night, the Holy Spirit began to convict me of my selfishness. I could have given him a few dollars to buy food, but I did not. I could have taken a greater interest in him, but I did not. I could have prayed with him, but again, I did not. I extended mercy, but I withheld the hand of Grace. God never does that. Our heavenly Father is always more than merciful, He always abounds with Grace.

Concerning our faith, James warns that failure to use our faith will cause it to become dormant. It was not a dormant faith that drove us to accept the Grace of God, it was an active faith. So, He now asks, "Can that type of faith save us?" The answer of course is, "No." A dormant faith will drive no one to Jesus. How sad is that? Jesus said, *"You will know them by their fruits"* (see Matt. 7:15-20).

God will often bring people into our lives who need monetary help as a way of testing both our faith and our obedience. Someone has said, "If God can get money through you, He will be sure and get it to you." Jesus warned in a parable that if we have the means to help others and fail to do so, that we may be closing the door of blessings that God intended for us to enjoy (see Matt 13:12). God's kingdom is all about sowing and reaping. James is reminding us that extending a helping hand is a wonderful way to love on people and allow God to love on us. God will never be indebted to anyone, so He continually sows innumerable blessings into the lives of sowers and givers. There will always be abundant seed for the sower, and there will always be sufficient food for the eater. He does not demand that we give and sow into every need, for that is impossible, but when His Spirit nudges us to give, we need to cheerfully do so.

Vs. 18: *[18] But someone may well say, "You have faith and I have works; show me your faith without the works, and I will show you my faith by my works."*

We can talk the talk, but unless we are producing fruit, we are not walking the walk. Ralph Waldo Emerson was quoted as saying, "What you do speaks so loudly that I cannot hear what you say." Jesus said it another way, *"So then, you will know them by their fruits"* (Matt. 7:20). A good fruit tree will, in time, bear good fruit. The fig tree that Jesus cursed can be compared to those who profess Christianity but are barren of fruit.

Vs. 19-23: *¹⁹ You believe that God is one. You do well; the demons also believe, and shudder. ²⁰ But are you willing to recognize, you foolish fellow, that faith without works is useless? ²¹ Was not Abraham our father justified by works when he offered up Isaac his son on the altar? ²² You see that faith was working with his works, and as a result of the works, faith was perfected; ²³ and the Scripture was fulfilled which says, "And Abraham believed God, and it was reckoned to him as righteousness," and he was called the friend of God.*

Believing that God can save us and receiving His Son Jesus for salvation are not one and the same. Believing is not enough. As a young person I understood that I was a sinner, but for many years I held tightly to the back of a pew when the Holy Spirit was convicting me. Finally, a night came when I could resist no longer. No, I did not go to the altar, but there in my seat I received God's miracle-working mercy and grace into my heart. Once again, believing and receiving are not one and the same. How about you, dear reader, are you sure of your salvation? You can be, for Romans 8:16 declares, *"The Spirit Himself testifies with our spirit that we are children of God."*

After receiving salvation, the average Christian does not truly understand that their old man has been crucified with Christ (Romans 6:6), so let's talk about it.

We were all born with a sin nature because we are descendants of Adam. However, our old man, our sin nature, was crucified with Christ (see Romans 6:6). Not only was our sin nature crucified with Christ, but our spirit person was quickened to life. The Father said of the prodigal son, *"for this son of mine was dead and has come to life again"* (Luke 15:24). That is what happened to us. God breathed into us the spirit of life, and our spirit person came alive.

Before salvation, our soul person was destined for hell, but Jesus came rushing to the rescue. *"For He rescued us from the domain of darkness, and transferred us to the kingdom of His beloved Son"* (Col.1:13). Yet, here is the quagmire for most of the Christian Church. We at times still wrestle with the issue of sin. Once again, let's be reminded that our mind did not get saved when we said yes to Jesus. Our heart, mind, and soul are not one and the same. They all live in one body, but our soul and our mind are not one and the same. The only hope for our unsaved mind is to renew it with the Word of God (see Romans 12:2). The hearing of the Word is the power that increases our faith.

The works of Abraham that James refers to did not thrive in his heart because he sat down and waited for Elijah's chariot to show up and take him into heaven. It came because he placed his faith and trust in God to fulfill His promise. He moved in humble obedience when God commanded him to take his only son Isaac to Mount Moriah to be slain as a living sacrifice. Abraham spoke to his servants and said, *"Stay here with the donkey, and I and the lad will go over there; and we will worship and return to you."* (Gen. 22:5). Take careful notice of his words, because they are faith-filled words. Abraham was convinced that they would both go up, and that they would both return. Abraham believed that God would raise his son from the dead, so he put his faith into action. He acted with faith, and God as always, met him at his point of faith. He will do the same for us. The Bible says, *"Even so Abraham believed God, and it was reckoned to him as righteous"* (Gal. 3:6). Before Abraham plunged his knife into the heart of young Isaac, God stopped him. Caught in a nearby thicket of thorns was a ram, God's provision to take the place of Abraham's son.

God chose to share this powerful story of faith with us because it is a picture of the coming Cross. It is a type and shadow of the sacrificial Lamb of God, a man named Jesus, born of a virgin named Mary. It was Jesus who would wear a crown of thorns and hang on an old rugged Cross as the atonement for the sins of the world. Abraham, the father of faith, looked forward to the Cross with veiled eyes. We look back at the Cross with greater clarity because the veil has been removed.

Vs. 24-26: *[24] You see that a man is justified by works and not by faith alone. [25] In the same way, was not Rahab the harlot also justified by works when she received the messengers and sent them out by another way? [26] For just as the body without the spirit is dead, so also faith without works is dead.*

It has been said that in most groups and clubs that require membership, twenty percent of the people usually do eighty percent of the work. Unfortunately, those numbers hold true in our Lord's Church as well. But here is a greater truth: God did not save us to become bench warmers. He saved us and equipped us to be involved in the game of life, especially in the life of His Church. James had seen far too many bench warmers, so he drew a comparison between them and Rahab the Harlot. Guess who lost. Yep, you are right, it was the bench warmers, and they are still losing today.

It bears mentioning that this same Rahab, who made her living as a harlot, is also listed in the Hebrew, "Faith Hall of Fame" (see Heb. 11:31). Rahab knew very little of Jehovah, but all of Jericho had heard that Israel's God was mightier than their gods. They had heard that the God of Israel had saved His people by destroying the mighty army of Egypt. Having heard of this great God, she did not abandon the possibility that He might one day save her from her horrific life as well. Upon hearing that Israel and their God were coming up against the people of Jericho, the little flame that was inside began to blaze ever brighter. Believing that the God of Israel would save her and her family, Rahab was willing to risk her own life by hiding two Hebrew men on the roof of her home. When the Canaanite warriors came searching for the Hebrew men, she lied and told them they had gone out of the gate. *"Pursue them quickly!"* she said. There may be others, but her lie is the only one I can recall that God has chosen to honor. Rahab's decision turned out to be a very wise decision. Against all odds, the walls of Jericho fell flat and those inside became victims of Israel's onslaught, all but Rahab and her family. They alone were saved.

It is also interesting that this woman, whose means of support was one of harlotry, is named in the lineage of Jesus. She was assimilated into the tribe of Israel when she married an Israelite named Salmon, of the tribe of Judah.

She gave birth to a child named Boaz. Boaz, another type and shadow of our Redeemer, redeemed a young widow named Ruth, and the rest is history.

Not understanding the magnitude of God's grace, most of us would have disqualified Rahab, but God's mercy and grace cannot be contained by sin. *"Where sin increased, grace abounded all the more"* (Rom. 5:20). This is a good time to pause and give praise unto our Savior, that in our own lives, that every time we sin, the grace of God abounds all the more. God's grace is never a license to sin, but rather, it is an empowerment to not sin. God forgave Rahab of her sinful past and decreed that her future would be clothed in glory. Dear Reader, He will do the same for you. Of this we can be sure, we cannot allow our faith to become dormant. Real faith sees past the obstacles. Real faith always sees the way. Real faith cannot be contained. With God's help, it will accomplish that for which it was given. Real faith is always moving from glory to glory, producing good fruit as it travels the roads of life.

JAMES
CHAPTER THREE

Vs. 1-2: *¹Let not many of you become teachers, my brethren, knowing that as such we will incur a stricter judgment. ²For we all stumble in many ways. If anyone does not stumble in what he says, he is a perfect man, able to bridle the whole body as well.*

Everyone in the body of Christ has been given a spiritual gift, but not everyone is gifted to teach the Scriptures. It is also worth noting that having the ability to teach secular knowledge does not automatically qualify a person to teach God's Word. There is a difference in physical talents and spiritual gifts. Physical talents are God-given talents that are ours upon birth and usually begin to manifest with age. Spiritual gifts are breathed into us by God at the time of our spiritual birth for the purpose of bringing increase to the Kingdom.

The apostle Peter reminds us, *"[No] prophecy of Scripture is a matter of one's own interpretation"* (2 Peter 1:20), while the apostle Paul reveals another profound truth: *"a natural [unsaved] man does not accept the things of the Spirit of God, for they are foolishness to him"* (1 Cor. 2:14 bracketed word added). By contrast, every born-again believer can glean from Scripture because they have the counsel of the Holy Spirit living in them. Every teacher who has taught for any length of time has learned that not all Christians have a hunger for the Word of God. However, those whom God has anointed to teach will impart seeds of truth that will, in time, bear fruit, even in those who seem to be zoned out and inattentive to the Word.

James reinforces the seriousness of handling God's Word with this warning in James 3:1: *"Let not many of you become teachers, my brethren, knowing that as such we will incur a stricter judgment."* Why will teachers incur a stricter judgment? James gives us greater insight in Chapter Four when he reminds every Christian, *"Therefore to him that knoweth to do good, and doeth it not, to him it is sin"* (James 4:17). In other words, teachers should know more, with exception, than those who are not teachers. Therefore, teachers will be held to a higher standard, not only in the way they handle the Word, but in their lives as well. Everyone should strive to live an exemplary life, but teachers even more so.

Several years ago, my wife and I decided to enjoy a night out at the movies. At the time, our small-town theater could only show two movies at a time, but we were impressed that we had a choice. On this particular night, one movie was rated R and the other G. As we were leaving the theater, a group of teenagers were exiting at another door. They all waved, but one young man took time to come over and speak. He said, "Mr. Don, we were all watching to see if you and Miss Penny were going to the R movie or the G movie." My wife and I do not go to R-rated movies, and not to sound angelic, but we avoid most PG movies as well. I made that comment in one of our Bible study groups, and someone responded, "You don't get to go see many movies if all you can go to are G and a few PG movies." Our response? "Sad but true." We enjoy movies, but we learned that we cannot subject ourselves to the lewd language and innuendos that many PG movies present to its audiences. Anyone who believes they can is greatly deceived. What message would we have sent to those youngsters had they seen us go into an R-rated movie?

Many Christians, including teachers of the Word, have an inward dread of standing before the Judgment Seat of Christ. Their fear is based on the belief that they will be judged for their sins, but what do the Scriptures say? Paul wrote, *"For we must all appear before the judgment seat of Christ, so that each one may be recompensed for his deeds in the body, according to what he has done, whether good or bad"* (2 Cor. 5:10). To be recompensed is to receive payment, not judgment.

Hebrews 9:27-28, *"And inasmuch as it is appointed for men to die once and after this comes judgment, so Christ also, having been offered once to bear the sins of many, will appear a second time for salvation without reference to sin, to those who eagerly await Him."* Thankfully, believers will not stand before Christ to account for their sins because Jesus bore the judgment for all sin on the Cross of Calvary. However, every believer will stand before Him and give an account for their lives.

As we stand before His judgment seat, our lives here on earth will come to light. Every deed will be examined, and for those that were done with purity of heart, we will receive crowns. Every good deed we did with impure motives will be burned as wood, hay, and stubble. I suspect there will be a lot of smoke going up. Yet, we can take heart. It is here that we will receive the one crown that stands out above all other crowns, the Crown of Life. When our Lord places that crown on our heads, we will long to hear Him say, *"Well done, good and faithful servant"* (Matt. 25:23 NKJV). Jesus made it clear when He told the parable of the talents that the more He gives to His children, the more He expects in return.

Paul knew that the teaching of God's Word was the rock bed of Christian growth, so he wrote a letter to a young preacher named Timothy with these instructions, *"Be diligent to present yourself approved to God as a workman who does not need to be ashamed, accurately handling* [dividing] *the word of truth"* (2 Tim. 2:15 bracketed word added). Teachers of secular knowledge are important and greatly needed, but no teacher has greater relevancy to life than those who teach God's Word. God's Word is life, and it has the power to change lives.

Before moving on from the subject of teachers, let me issue a word of caution! Teachers of the Word must be careful of the books, commentaries, and other resources they use when preparing a lesson. For instance, reading the works of Flavius Josephus and other historians is interesting and informative, but their work should never be presented as truth. Facts and truth are not one and the same, and a little leaven goes a long way. Facts tend to change, but the Word of God (truth) is unchanging. That does not mean that we cannot glean from the thoughts and insights of sources other than the Bible, but God's Word, and God's Word alone, has the power to give life and change lives (see Heb. 4:12).

Vs. 3-6: *³Now if we put the bits into the horses' mouths so that they will obey us, we direct their entire body as well. ⁴ Look at the ships also, though they are so great and are driven by strong winds, are still directed by a very small rudder wherever the inclination of the pilot desires. ⁵ So also the tongue is a small part of the body, and yet it boasts of great things. See how great a forest is set aflame by such a small fire! ⁶ And the tongue is a fire, the very world of iniquity; the tongue is set among our members as that which defiles the entire body, and sets on fire the course of our life, and is set on fire by hell.*

James is passionate about many aspects of Christian behavior, but none more so than Christian tongues that are out of control. He had witnessed firsthand the damage of uncontrolled tongues at work, so he confronts the issue by using animals, ships, and campfires to make his point. We have all witnessed the enormous fires that have plagued our beautiful country because someone was careless with a campfire. Never would these campers have dreamed that their small fire would cause the loss of millions of acres of good trees, beautiful homes, and more importantly, human lives. In the same way, Satan can take a few words spoken in anger or jealousy and use them to divide entire churches, communities, homes, and marriages.

One of the greatest and most profound truths of Scripture is found in Proverbs 18:21, *"Death and life are in the power of the tongue."* This truth is seldom taught in most churches, but thankfully, that is beginning to change. If we listen closely to those going through unpleasant trials, we will usually discover that they are constantly verbalizing their woes and problems. That is akin to trying to put out a fire with gas instead of water. The answer to the tests and trials we find ourselves in is never to agree with the problems, but rather, to speak God's Word and promises. We should not be in denial that a problem exists, but we should always deny its right to exist. Be forewarned, conquering our tongue is not an overnight victory. It is a lifelong quest. It takes knowledge, training, and determination, but we must learn to speak God's Word and promises to the mountain and stop agreeing with the problem.

Jesus said, *"For by your words you will be justified, and by your words you will be condemned"* (Matt. 12:37). We need to stop and meditate on those words for a moment because they are pivotal to the success of our Christian walk. Jesus said that our words have the power to justify, and our words have the power to condemn. No right-thinking person wants to live in condemnation, and every right-thinking person wants to be justified in the eyes of God.

So why do so many Christians unwittingly live under condemnation instead of justification? Everyone has an opinion, but it may well be that most of the body of Christ have never been taught that there is life and death in the power of their tongues. Due to a lack of knowledge we say things such as, "No good deed will go unpunished," or, "If it weren't for bad luck, I'd have no luck at all," or, "It's flu season. I always get the flu," or, "There is always more month than money." These clichés may sound cute and harmless, but harmless they are not. Words spoken can prove to be very prophetic, bringing life or death.

Let's face it, all of us slip and say negative things, but to daily saturate the airwaves with negative words is a recipe for living under condemnation and negative circumstances. We must train ourselves to say words such as, "Lord, I thank You that I walk in health, and everything I put my hands to prospers" (see 3 John 2), or, *"The Lord is my Shepherd, I shall not want"* (Ps. 23:1). By the way, dear Christian, it is not that David's cup was half empty or half full. David declared that his cup was running over.

Consider carefully that Jesus did not defeat Satan with thoughts, He defeated the evil one with words. In the same way, we too gain victory by speaking the written Word. Conversely, the very opposite is birthed when we speak words of doubt and fear. Job said, *"For what I fear comes upon me, and what I dread befalls me"* (Job 3:25). Job had allowed his inward fears to become the master of his tongue and his actions. God did not put a hole in his shield of protection. Job allowed the enemy entrance into his life through fear. Thoughts of fear must be conquered with spoken words of faith.

God's Word is not subject to political correctness, nor was it meant to be. Wisdom says that political correctness must stand the test of God's Word, not the other way around. God's Word is established and unchanging, while facts are constantly changing.

In centuries past, it was an accepted fact that the world was flat. Had the wisdom of the world been willing to listen to God's prophet Isaiah, science would have known that the earth was not flat. *"It is He who sits above the circle of the earth"* (Is. 40:22). Fools will always scoff at God, but scoff as they may, facts will never be greater than God's truth. Of this we can be sure, our Heavenly Father will never lower His Laws of morality to accommodate immoral lifestyles.

Vs. 7-12: *⁷For every species of beasts and birds, of reptiles and creatures of the sea, is tamed and has been tamed by the human race. ⁸But no one can tame the tongue; it is a restless evil and full of deadly poison. ⁹ With it we bless our Lord and Father, and with it we curse men, who have been made in the likeness of God; ¹⁰ from the same mouth come both blessing and cursing. My brethren, these things ought not to be this way. ¹¹Does a fountain send out from the same opening both fresh and bitter water? ¹² Can a fig tree, my brethren, produce olives, or a vine produce figs? Nor can salt water produce fresh.*

James may come across as somewhat stern, and at times he does speak rather sternly, but he always does so in Christian love. Every good parent will at various times issue a stern warning to their children, but they do so to keep them from suffering harm, not because they do not love them. In these verses, James warns about the power of words by painting word pictures of untamed animals and compares their unwillingness to be tamed with our own tongues.

In many churches, there is no ground as hallowed as that of tradition, but there are times when truth will belie certain traditions. There are also times when truth runs head on into the doctrines of men. Beware, for there are many unsound doctrines out there. Even the most ardent of teachers will at times err in their interpretation of certain Scriptures. The apostle Paul was right on when he said, *"For now we see in a mirror dimly, but then face to face"* (1 Cor. 13:12). Paul is saying that we can know a lot, but we will not know everything on this side of heaven. That is why we need to always search Scripture for ourselves and ask God to reveal His Word to us. Of this we can be sure, any teacher who has never erred and knows much about everything has a lot to learn.

The love James has for his fellow brothers and sisters in Christ is the same manner of love we should always strive to exhibit. We who are new creations in Christ Jesus should be careful that we do not speak in love and forgiveness one minute and anger and malice the next. A double-minded tongue is very confusing to the unsaved world, to new Christians, and to our own minds as well. We need to daily remind ourselves that we are the only Bible that many people will ever read.

If you have never read the Book of Genesis, please consider doing so. It is chock-full of marvelous events and miracles that help us understand the sovereignty of God. Not only that, but Genesis is foundational in helping us understand all other Scriptures. The first three chapters alone bring His creation to life and set us on a pathway of hungering for His Word. It is here that we see God giving Adam complete dominion over the earth and every living creature.

Before sin entered the picture, the earth was void of earthquakes, the weather was always perfect, and wild animals were herbivores. In summation, man was in complete harmony with God, and everything on earth was in complete harmony with man. There was no worry, no anxiety, and no fear. In fact, Adam and Eve knew zero about the emotion of fear. Eve was secure in every way, so she was not at all frightened when a snake showed up and began a conversation.

She may have been amazed that such a creature could talk, but fear was not an issue. Not one animal created by God would have harmed her, but everything changed when she and Adam disobeyed God's commandment. With sin came the curse, causing the seas to rage, the earth to belch, and wild animals to thirst for blood. As any animal trainer will attest, wild animals are not easy to train, and they can never be completely trusted.

For this reason, James makes an eye-opening comparison. Man has been able to tame the fiercest of beasts, but he is unable to tame his own tongue. Verse eight sounds as though the taming of our tongue is impossible, and without God, it is impossible. The good news is that we are not without God because His Spirit dwells in us. Our flesh cannot tame the volatility of our unruly tongue, but the Holy Spirit can. The Holy Spirit who resides in us is well able to tame any tongue, even the vilest of tongues.

Vs. 13-16: *¹³Who among you is wise and understanding? Let him show by his good behavior his deeds in the gentleness of wisdom. ¹⁴ But if you have bitter jealousy and selfish ambition in your heart, do not be arrogant and so lie against the truth. ¹⁵ This wisdom is not that which comes down from above, but is earthly, natural, demonic. ¹⁶ For where jealousy and selfish ambition exist, there is disorder and every evil thing.*

James began his letter by confirming to the Church that God will liberally give His wisdom to anyone who seeks for it in faith. What is the essence of God's wisdom? It is everything that is good and saturated with love. But as James acknowledges, there are many Christians whom God has set free in the spirit who still live their lives in the flesh. Hearts that are filled with jealousy and unforgiveness are hearts that are drowning in deceit.

Verse fifteen contains revelation knowledge that clearly exposes the schemes of our enemy, Satan. James reveals that there are two types of wisdom. One belongs to the kingdom of Darkness, the other to the Kingdom of Light. One is the true wisdom of God, while the other is a wisdom whose foundation is built on sand. In truth, the world's wisdom is not wisdom at all because it is always based on what can be seen, on lies and deception. Let me reiterate, deception is believing that a lie is truth, or believing that a fact is superior to God's Word. Millions of lives have run amuck and been destroyed because people followed the wisdom of the world instead of God's Word.

Vs. 17-18: *¹⁷But the wisdom from above is first pure, then peaceable, gentle, reasonable, full of mercy and good fruits, unwavering, without hypocrisy. ¹⁸ And the seed whose fruit is righteousness is sown in peace by those who make peace.*

It would be very easy to sail past these last two verses in search of what lies ahead in Chapter Four, but that would be like leaving one rich diamond field in search of another. These two verses contain the fruits of life that we all desire to enjoy. More than anything else, we all desire to live in peace and harmony, so let's take a moment to examine the life that Christ Jesus died to give us. As we examine the fruits that are the harvest of godly wisdom, let's compare them to the fruit that now exists in our homes, our marriages, and every other facet of our lives.

Let's begin by defining what godly wisdom really is. First and foremost, God's wisdom, unlike the wisdom of the world, is pure. In other words, God's wisdom is absolutely perfect in every way. It contains no blemishes, no ifs, buts, or maybes. Conversely, purity is foreign to the makeup of worldly wisdom. Worldly wisdom has its own agenda, with the end result being some type of personal gain. Now let's contrast that to the wisdom of God's Word found in Proverbs 16:16: *"How much better it is to get wisdom than gold! And to get understanding is to be chosen above silver."* That is not the mindset or agenda of worldly wisdom that permeates the thoughts and goals of the unsaved world. Neither is it the mindset of the unsaved alone. It is also the mindset of many Christians.

Having read God's Word, let's get honest with ourselves.

If it were possible to put God's wisdom in a box, and place it next to two other larger boxes that were filled with the purest of gold and silver, which would you choose?

Do you know which one most of us would choose? Of course, you do. Most of us would choose the gold. That is why there is not enough of God's wisdom in the hearts of most Christians. We are more consumed with the things of the world than we are with God's Kingdom. We would reason that we can take the box of gold and serve God at the same time. Jesus said, not so, *"You cannot serve God and wealth"* (Matt. 6:24). God is not opposed to His children having wealth, but He is opposed to wealth having us.

In 1 Kings 3:5, God said to Solomon, *"Ask what you wish me to give you."* God offered Solomon anything his heart desired, but Solomon replied, *"Give Your servant an understanding heart to judge Your people to discern between good and evil. For who is able to judge this great people of Yours?"* In other words, Solomon sought wisdom from God above all the riches the world could offer. Because he did, God caused immeasurable wealth to flow to him, so much so that he became the wealthiest man of all the ages.

Having been enriched beyond measure because he sought godly wisdom, Solomon turned his heart to the wisdom of the world. Many Christians do that. They start out with God, but as they are blessed, they stop seeking after God. That was the road that King Solomon took, and his life ended in misery and chaos. Too late, he discovered that his wealth could purchase things that gave temporary pleasure, but it could not purchase love, joy, or peace. Solomon proclaimed, *"So I hated life, for the work which had been done under the sun was grievous to me; because everything is futility and striving after wind"* (Eccl. 2:17).

God's wisdom offers peace without measure, and it is free for the taking, yet millions of Christians cannot go to sleep at night unless they have some type of sleep aid. They continually wrestle with anxiety, worry, and fear because they live their lives in the wisdom of the world. No pill available on the market today can take those maladies away, but godly wisdom can.

Jesus lived in the same world of turmoil as we, but His life was the persona of peace. He was gentle, yet strong, continually using the foolish things of the world to confound the wise. God is not looking for men and women who have Ph.D.s, hanging on their walls. He is looking for people of all ages who hunger for His wisdom.

Mercy, good fruits, and steadfastness are but a few of the serendipities that God has supplied for us through His atonement given at the Cross. They are ours for the asking, but they will not manifest in our lives until we are willing to meet His conditions. What are His conditions? *"Seek first His kingdom and His righteousness, and all these things will be added to you"* (Matt. 6:33).

Finally, we need to stop seeking for something that Christ Jesus has already given to us. He has already given us every spiritual blessing in the heavenly places. He has given us His peace and He has robed us in His righteousness. The Blood was supplied at Calvary. Now it is up to us to make sure that we daily apply it to our lives.

~ JAMES ~
CHAPTER FOUR

Vs. 1-3: *¹ What is the source of quarrels and conflicts among you? Is not the source your pleasures that wage war in your members? ² You lust and do not have; so you commit murder. You are envious and cannot obtain; so you fight and quarrel. You do not have because you do not ask. ³ You ask and do not receive, because you ask with wrong motives, so that you may spend it on your pleasures.*

If anyone is searching for a little relief from some of the issues addressed in Chapter Three, they will surely be disappointed with Chapter Four. I use the word "disappointed" with tongue in cheek because every believer knows that the truth is the only thing that will set us free. We need to remind ourselves that the quarrels and conflicts we see in some churches did not begin at church. They began in the hearts of those in conflict, at home, in marriages, and relationships.

We can understand why those who are without Christ talk and act in unbecoming ways because that is their nature. But the same cannot be said of we who are in Christ. James is saying in no uncertain terms that God's people should not behave as the unsaved world behaves. Having walked with Christ, we should also have matured and taken on the attributes of Christ, taking seriously the words of James when he said, *"My brethren, these things ought not to be this way"* (James 3:10).

The apostle Paul wrote in 1 Corinthians 2:14, *"A natural man does not accept the things of the Spirit of God, for they are foolishness to him; and he cannot understand them, because they are spiritually appraised."* James is saying, "Wake up Church! Stop being a hypocrite. Stop acting like the world acts. Get a revelation. That is no longer who you are! You are new creations in Christ Jesus" (my interjection). One thing we know for sure, James is willing to deal with these issues head on, making no attempt to sweep them under the rug.

Agreeing to disagree can, at times, be expected, but disagreements that are not disarmed with Christian love will always fan flames of strife and disharmony. It takes maturing Christians to say, "I am sorry," when they are wrong. But it takes a mature Christian to apologize and say, "I am sorry," when it is evident that the other person is wrong. One thing is certain, James is right when he concludes that being carnally minded is the major source of all quarrels and conflicts. The lust James is referring to is not necessarily sexual lust but a selfish lust that demands "my way or the highway," or "You have encroached onto my territory."

While James may seem extreme when he refers to murder as the outcome of fighting and quarrels, allow me to share a memorable event that was seared into my memory bank.

I was attending a men's Christian conference with one of my sons. Our meetings took place in a large theater type building that held several hundred men. During one of the conference sessions, one of the speakers, being full of the Holy Spirit, received a word of knowledge, so he suddenly stopped teaching and said, "God has shown me that one of you came to this conference with a plan to murder his wife. I want that man to stand up and come up on stage." Too no one's surprise, no one moved. In fact, we were shocked that he had made such a statement. Certain that he had received a word of knowledge, he repeated his challenge, but again, no one moved. Refusing to let the issue go, he said, "God has shown me that there is a man here who is planning to kill his wife, and He has shown me who you are. If you do not come forward I am coming to get you." Moments seemed like eternity, but seated close by was a tall, lanky man. Slowly, he arose from his seat and made his way to the stage. Who would have dreamed it? In the middle of several hundred men seeking a closer walk with the Lord was a man who planned to murder his wife. Yet, there he stood on stage, openly confessing that he intended to murder his wife. Laying hands on him, they prayed for his deliverance from evil spirits.

Thankfully, most Christians would never contemplate physical murder, but those numbers increase substantially when consideration is given to murder with words. We must not be deceived, words can kill. Neither can we allow ourselves to be deceived by the world's wisdom. When we do, we allow the curse that is in the world to affect the course of our lives. Lack in some form, not necessarily money, is always the result. Worldly wisdom always asks for selfish reasons. Godly wisdom asks for the right reasons. While God is our faithful Father who greatly desires to meet our needs, He is not obligated to answer selfish prayers in the affirmative.

Vs. 4-5: *⁴You adulteresses, do you not know that friendship with the world is hostility toward God? Therefore whoever wishes to be a friend of the world makes himself an enemy of God. ⁵ Or do you think that the Scripture speaks to no purpose: "He jealously desires the Spirit which He has made to dwell in us"?*

James is using the term "adulteress" in the same way that many of the Old Testament prophets used the term. It was a warning to the Israelites who had rejected God and replaced Him with pagan gods and practices. Fast forward to the twenty-first century, and we find that Satan's tactics have not changed. He is using every deceiving lie at his disposal to create a new code of morality within the Bride of Christ, God's Church. Worldly wisdom says that Christians are wrong if they do not embrace adultery, fornication, and same-sex marriages as acceptable lifestyles. The key word being pushed is "Tolerance." Tolerance meaning that we must accept everyone, regardless of how they act, what they say, or what they think. Tolerance in that sense of the word is not scriptural. It is sad but true that a growing segment of the Christian Church has embraced this line of thinking. Adultery, fornication, homosexuality, vulgar speech, and coarse jesting are but a few of the immoral lifestyles that we are told we must tolerate. We who are the Church can tolerate a lot of things, but those who push a so-called progressive lifestyle want far more than tolerance of their behavior. They are demanding that Christians "accept and incorporate" such behavior into the Church. Not one writer of any Book of the Bible believed that we should tolerate such behavior. Jesus never gave a nod of acceptance to sin. He loved the sinner, but He hated sin. The apostle Paul, as well as Peter, John, and Jude wrote and warned against such behavior.

When it was reported that a man who professed Christianity was living with his father's wife, Paul openly rebuked the local church for its failure to address the situation (see 1 Cor. 5). The old cliché, "we must be tolerant" is one of Satan's strongest tools as he goes about his business of attempting to destroy God's Church and remove every vestige of godly restraint from society. Anyone who believes that God is tolerant of sin needs to spend some time looking at the old rugged Cross. Jesus died for all, for every sin named, but He did not endure the agony of the Cross to embrace our sins. We all sin in different ways, even after receiving God's grace for our salvation, but a truly repentant Christian will not continue in a lifestyle of open sin. Sheep do not willingly live in hog pens because that is not their nature.

Isaiah 1:18 states: *"Come now, and let us reason together,"* says the Lord, *"though your sins are as scarlet, they will be as white as snow; though they are red like crimson, they will be like wool."* God has not changed His mind. He is still willing to reason with us, but He is not willing to compromise with us. None of this is to say that we do not want people who are living openly immoral lifestyles to attend church. No, just the opposite. We want those who are living immoral lifestyles to feel welcome in the church. The last thing they need is a cold shoulder from Christian brothers and sisters. However, we should never be deceived into believing that Church membership should be offered those in immoral lifestyles as defined by God's Word. The goal of Satan is to remove every moral restraint, not some but *all* moral restraint. To accomplish his goal, he knows that he must first gain membership. Once membership has been granted, he is free to move his disciples into roles of leadership, and from there to the pulpit.

The Laodicean Church will be the church that abandons the moral absolutes of God and embraces sin openly. They will do so on the premise of "Tolerance," but the real reason for their tolerance is this: they do not accept the Bible as the infallible, inerrant, Word of God. If the Bible in totality cannot be trusted as truth to all generations, then no part of it can be trusted. Such a Bible will become our enemies' strongest tool. It will no longer be considered as God's inerrant Word that was breathed through prophets and men of God to His people. It will simply become another book on a bookshelf.

James uses the same sobering analogy in these verses to remind us that behaving in an ungodly manner severely limits God's promises that are every believer's rich inheritance. "What is going on in my life?" we ask. If our lives seem chaotic and full of strife, we might take a good look at the things we have tolerated and allowed into our hearts. The enemy wants us to believe that God has cut off His promises because we have sinned, but that is not the way His Kingdom works. The truth is that we cannot live in unrepentant sin and walk in abundant faith at the same time. It is impossible. Our enemy knows this truth all too well, so he seizes on those with weak faith who are perishing from lack of the Word and says, "God is no longer pleased with you." Do not believe him. He is a liar and the father of lies. The river of favor and protection does not ebb and flow because we have sinned or not sinned. It always flows the same. The river of favor may appear to have dried up, but it is not because our Heavenly Father has chosen to cut off the flow. It is usually because we have walked out from under God's umbrella of protection. At other times it may be because of circumstances that are beyond our control, but even then, there are no circumstances that God cannot cause to work together for our good. We have any enemy who loves to create chaos and lack, but it is not our Heavenly Father.

This may be a good opportunity to remind ourselves that Satan did not present the first issue of *Better Homes and Gardens* at your home address. The first edition went to an estate called, "The Garden of Eden." However, the enticements remain the same. It brought failure and sorrow to Adam and Eve, and it will do the same to us. Somehow, along the way, many Christians have bought into the lie that we can continue in sin and not suffer a consequence. Nothing could be further from the truth.

Caution! Grace does cover every sin of a believer, but Grace is not a guarantee that the knock we hear at our door is not an unwanted consequence. Unrepentant sin always gives birth to negative consequences. While sin no longer has the power to separate a believer from God, God will not be mocked. His law of "sowing and reaping" is irrevocable. Unless God chooses to intercede and stand in the way of Satan's trap of destruction, we will reap what we sow. He has interceded for all of us at various times and chosen to cover our sin. For those times we give thanks. But we would have to admit that until we chose to repent and forsake our sin, we found ourselves living far below the blessings He wants us to enjoy.

Verse five makes it clear that God placed His Holy Spirit inside us for His purpose and our well-being. God miraculously took His children out of Egypt, but it was no small task to get Egypt out of His children. In fact, thousands of them died in the desert because they insisted on trusting in the gods of Egypt. They wanted God's promises, but they failed to receive them because they lacked in faith. That is being double-minded, and God says that such a person will receive nothing from Him. God's restraints were not to keep Israel from enjoying life. They were given to assure them that they could enjoy life.

We are no different. That is why the apostle Paul wrote, *"He who began a good work in you will perfect it until the day of Jesus"* (Phil. 1:6). The Holy Spirit is constantly at work in us, but the worries and cares of the world often drown out His voice. The dawning of each day brings with it a bundle of individual choices. It is up to us. Which voice will we listen to? Who will we live for? Joshua said, *"Choose for yourselves today whom you will serve"* (Josh. 24:15). God chose to save us, but the strength and power of our relationship with Him from that point on is our choice entirely.

Concerning verse five, Ezekiel prophesied, *"And I will*

give you a new heart and put a new spirit within you" (Ez. 36:26). A man by the name of Nicodemus was clueless concerning this great prophecy. In love, Jesus asked of him, *"Are you the teacher of Israel and do not understand these things?"* (John 3:10). No, he did not understand Ezekiel's prophecy, but the same should not be said of born-again children of God. Nicodemus was looking forward to the Cross, but we have the luxury of looking back at the Cross. We can see with great clarity the victory that Jesus won at the Cross, for we have been given *"the Mind of Christ"* (1 Cor. 2:16). *"Your word is a lamp to my feet and a light to my path"* (Ps. 119:105). Because of this great truth, the same distinctive difference that separated Jesus from the religious Pharisees should be mirrored in our lives as well.

Vs. 6-7: *⁶ But He gives a greater grace. Therefore, it says, "God is opposed to the proud, but gives grace to the humble." ⁷ Submit therefore to God. Resist the devil and he will flee from you.*

The greater grace spoken of here is Jesus Himself. There is no greater mercy than God's mercy, and there is no greater grace than God's grace. Neither His mercy nor His grace were given to us because we deserved or earned them. Quite the contrary. God gave them to us because He loves us. Many Christians have a tough time with this, but Grace is not a gift that is being doled out to us based on our goodness or works. His gifts of mercy and grace are ours because of the finished work of Jesus. It has zero to do with our performance. God's grace cannot be measured, but rather, it is given to us without measure. If we are not walking in abundant grace, it is probably because we are walking according to our flesh and not the Spirit.

Many Christians attempt to walk in the Spirit, but they fail miserably because they have failed to adhere to one very basic truth. We must submit to the Lord and then resist the devil. Attempting to resist the devil before we submit every facet of our life to the Lord is another recipe for failure. It is no wonder that there are so many miserable Christians. Self-effort and refusal to surrender all to the Lord are not paths to victory. Try as we may, we cannot resist Satan in our own power, and wisdom shouts, "Don't try!" Attempting to resist Satan in our own strength is foolish. Let's be clear, our part is not to defeat Satan. Satan has already been defeated. Our part is to walk according to the Spirit and not our flesh. Jesus said, *"This is the work of God, that you believe in Him whom He has sent"* (John 6:29).

Jesus defeated Satan soundly when He left the Cross, walked into hell and stripped him completely of power. Satan does not want us to know it, but he no longer has power over death, hell, and the grave. It is no wonder that he walks about as a roaring lion. His roar is far greater than his ability to bite. Jesus pulled his teeth and declawed him. His only hope is that God's children will stray into his web of deception that always begins with the lust of the eyes, the lust of the flesh, and the pride of life.

Vs. 8-10: *⁸ Draw near to God and He will draw near to you. Cleanse your hands, you sinners; and purify your hearts, you double-minded. ⁹ Be miserable and mourn and weep; let your laughter be turned into mourning and your joy to gloom. ¹⁰ Humble yourselves in the presence of the Lord, and He will exalt you.*

James is not talking about our position in Christ. He is talking about our relationship with Christ. We do not have to go on a long journey to draw near to God because He lives inside us. All we need to do is establish an open-door policy with Him. Jesus said, *"I am with you always, even to the end of the age"* (Matt. 28:20). Thankfully, the Holy Spirit who lives inside us does not come and go based on our actions. *"Do not grieve the Holy Spirit of God, by whom you were sealed for the day of redemption"* (Eph. 4:30).

The Holy Spirit longs to speak His supernatural wisdom into our natural minds. A mind changed by the Word of God no longer thinks as a double-minded person thinks. Quite the contrary. A mind changed by the Word of God thinks and speaks the Word of God. Jesus won His confrontation with Satan by speaking, *"It is written,"* and so will we. We must continually remind ourselves that we are the righteousness of God in Christ (see 2 Cor. 5:21). We must become resolute in the knowledge that our name has been written in the Lamb's Book of Life, and we must be resolute in God's promises that no power of hell can remove it.

Listen closely! When we do err and sin, the work of the Holy Spirit is not to condemn us. The work of the Holy Spirit is to convict us of our true identity in Christ, to remind us of who we are and whose we are. Condemnation drives us away from God. Conviction draws us back to God, reminding us of our position in Christ. We need to get this spiritual picture: We are seated with Him in heavenly places, and Jesus is guarding over our seats. James understood this spiritual truth, so we need to be clear that he was not condemning those who were causing conflict. He was, however, reminding them that acting in unbecoming ways would subject them to evil spirits.

Contrary to popular belief, there is no place in Scripture that says that the Holy Spirit condemns a born-again believer of sin. Just the opposite is found in Romans 8:1, *"Therefore there is now no condemnation for those who are in Christ Jesus."* Hard to swallow? For most Christians, it is hard to swallow. That is why many Christians live their lives in the shadows of condemnation, feeling unworthy in the eyes of God.

There are probably more, but I have listed below three major reasons that Christians struggle with condemnation.

1 - The first reason Christians feel condemned can be credited to our adversary Satan. Because of the Cross, the accuser can no longer go before the throne of God and accuse us when we err. When Jesus was on the Cross, He paid for our sins in full, past, present, and future. Therefore, Jesus, our strong Advocate, now stands in his way. So, what does he do? The accuser now comes directly to us and begins an attack against our minds. That is where spiritual war is now waged, in our minds. Satan is desperately trying to point us back to who we were and not allow us to focus on who we are now, the Righteousness of Christ. We were

sinners, and though we may at times sin, we are now the righteousness of God in Him (see 2 Cor. 5:21).

2 - The second reason Christians feel condemned are words of condemnation from people who live their lives under the Old Covenant of Law. "You do not measure up," they say. We must remind ourselves that their words are not true. Jesus said that we do measure up. He calls us sons and daughters, heirs of the King. When negative and condemning words come, remember the instructions of Jesus when He said, *"Take no thought, saying"* (Matt. 6:31 KJV). Consider carefully what He said. First, He tells us to reject the negative thought. Next, He instructs us to be sure that we do not speak those negative thoughts. Words are seeds that will produce what we say.

3 - The third reason is that we, at times, listen to the one person whose accusations hurt the most. Who could that be? We only need to look in a mirror to discover who that person is. It is the person looking back at us. No one is quicker to condemn us than ourselves. The accuser condemned Adam, so what did he attempt to do? He attempted to hide from God. That is what many Christians are doing today. Having fallen short once again, they attempt to hide from the Father, when all the time He is saying, *"Come to Me, all who are weary and heavy-laden, and I will give you rest"* (see Matt. 11:28-30). Yet, here is truth, *"Therefore if anyone is in Christ, he is a new creature; the old things passed away; behold, new things have come"* (2 Cor. 5:17).

The great evangelist Vance Havner, who went on to be with the Lord several years ago, preached many outstanding salvation messages. One sermon was titled, "Getting Accustomed To The Dark." The title always reminds me of the times I have gone to a movie theater. Several years back, my wife and I, along with another couple, went to see the movie "Jaws." The lights had been turned down when we entered the theater, and it was difficult to see. As we searched for seats, one of the most exhausting moments of the movie was taking place when my brother-in-law sat down in a lady's lap. She screamed, he screamed, and it seemed that everyone in the theater screamed. Apologizing profusely, we retreated to the wall and stood there until our eyes adjusted to the dark. In a few minutes, darkness was no longer an issue. We had become accustomed to the dark. Do you know anyone who has become accustomed to the dark? Pray that it is not ourselves.

In much the same way, James was warning members of the Church to wake up and open their spiritual eyes because they were acting and behaving in an unbecoming manor. None of us want to be pawns of the enemy, but we can allow ourselves to be used by him unless we are walking according to the Spirit. To keep this from happening, we must commit to spending time with the Lord. We need to confess that we have, at times, failed Him. We need to confess that our faith is not always what it needs to be, and we need to confess our need for Him. May I also add that true repentance will sometimes involve a little mourning and weeping. When the Lord shows up, His holiness will most certainly confront our flesh. In these blessed moments in time, weeping usually becomes a part of the encounter. When is the last time we wept before the Lord?

Vs. 11-12: *¹¹ Do not speak against one another, brethren. He who speaks against a brother, or judges his brother, speaks against the law and judges the Law; but if you judge the law, you are not a doer of the law but a judge of it. ¹² There is only one Lawgiver and Judge, the One who is able to save and to destroy; but who are you who judge your neighbor?*

Judging others is a subject that all of us must deal with from time to time. God gave the Law to Moses, and James is reminding us that the One who gave the Law is the only one capable of judging the heart and motives of another. However, judging another person should not be confused with the gift of spiritual discernment. God gives the spirit of discernment to every believer for a reason. He wants to keep us from being involved with wickedness and wicked people. Wickedness may be malicious gossip, or money schemes, or efforts to gain control, as in a church. A wise person will separate himself from these situations and these types of people. A wise person will also allow God to judge his heart and motives. When we judge others, we have pushed God out of His seat and taken it for ourselves. James is reminding us that we are not capable of rendering proper judgment. Jesus said, *"First take the log out of your own eye, and then you will see clearly to take the speck out of your brother's eye"* (Matt. 7:5).

The Law always demanded that a penalty be given to any person who broke the Law, and very often the penalty was death. James has already noted that when we revert to the Law and then fail to keep even the smallest point, we are guilty of all. If Jesus had used the Law as His measuring stick, the woman caught in adultery would have been stoned, and the Prodigal Son could not have returned home.

Vs. 13-17: *¹³ Come now, you who say, "Today or tomorrow, we shall go to such and such a city, and spend a year there and engage in business and make a profit." ¹⁴ Yet you do not know what your life will be like tomorrow. You are just a vapor that appears for a while and then vanishes away. ¹⁵ Instead, you ought to say, "If the Lord wills, we will live and also do this or that." ¹⁶ But as it is, you boast in your arrogance; all such boasting is evil. ¹⁷ Therefore, to one who know the right thing to do and does not do it, to him it is sin.*

Living on assumptions instead of godly knowledge is a sure recipe for disaster. Yet, many Christians live their lives that way. It is also the reason that many Christians find themselves in bad marriages, unfruitful jobs, and meaningless relationships. If that describes the way you feel or see life, let me give you this word of hope. We do not have to live a hopeless, unfulfilled life. All we need is an attitude change. God threw me a little nugget one time and said, "The problem is not with those who upset you. The problem is sitting in your chair." How true. When we decide to change, it is amazing that everything around us seems to change. He has predestined a great plan for our lives, but failure to come into agreement with His plan will keep us from fulfilling our God-given destiny.

Proverbs 16:25 warns, *"There is a way which seems right*

to a man, but its end is the way of death." The unsaved of this world live their lives based on feelings, and far too often Christians do the same. Notice carefully that God says what "seems right" is really the way of death. Following one's feelings has authored the death of countless marriages, invoked ill health, and robbed many of God's intended prosperity. Here is God's Word, and it is a good word, *"Commit your works to the Lord and your plans will be established"* (Prov. 16:3).

Young people are not the only ones who make bad choices, but they are too often the ones who start out in life on a wrong road. Why? Because they have not been trained to seek God's guidance for their future. Believers pray to God about marriage partners or job needs, but being double minded, many abandon His counsel and follow after their feelings. Can we know for certain that we are following God's plan? Yes, we can know for certain because God has made it possible. This is a great spiritual Truth: We can know because God is the only One who has the power to give perfect peace to our soul. Jesus said, *"Peace I leave with you; My peace I give to you; not as the world gives do I give to you"* (John 14:27). Satan can counterfeit circumstances and events, but he cannot counterfeit peace. No peace? God is saying, "No," or perhaps He is saying, "Wait." It may be God's desire for us, but the timing may not be right. Either way, a wise person will listen.

Jesus told a parable about a Certain Man who went down from Jerusalem to Jericho all alone. He was set upon by thieves who beat and robbed him, leaving him to die on the side of the road. Jesus always measured His every word, and He used the words, "Going down," to reference the effect of sin. Sin always takes us away from the Lord, which is exactly what happened to the man pictured here. He was safe in the Holy City of Jerusalem, but he chose to go down to the city of Jericho, a picture of sin. He traveled alone because it "seemed right." Of course, we know what happened. The enemy beat him, robbed him, and then left him to die. Thankfully, Jesus showed up, bandaged his wounds and took him to an inn for safety (picture of the Church).

Thanks be unto the Lord that no matter how bad we sometimes mess up, He is always willing to step in and clean us up. We can take solace in that, but how much better it would have been for the Certain Man if he had sought direction from the Lord before he set out on his journey. We faithfully sing the old hymn, "He Leadeth Me," but in truth, many of us should be singing, "He Follows Me." Had the Certain Man sought God in prayer before going on a journey, he would have heard the voice of the Holy Spirit saying, "Take Me with you," or "Don't go!" or perhaps, "Take another road." James says in verse 17, *"Therefore, to one who knows the right thing to do and does not do it, to him it is sin."*

JAMES CHAPTER FIVE

Vs. 1-6: *¹ Come now you rich, weep and howl, for your miseries which are coming upon you. ² Your riches have rotted and your garments have become moth-eaten. ³ Your gold and your silver have rusted; and their rust will be a witness against you and will consume your flesh like fire. ⁴ Behold, the pay of the laborers who mowed your fields, and which has been withheld by you, cries out against you; and the outcry of those who did the harvesting has reached the ears of the Lord of Sabbath. ⁵ You have lived luxuriously on the earth and led a life of wanton pleasure; you have fattened your hearts in a day of slaughter. ⁶ You have condemned and put to death the righteous man; he does not resist you.*

As we conclude the last chapter of the Book of James, keep in mind that this letter was primarily written to the born-again Jewish Church. Their culture was quite different from the world of the Gentiles that surrounded them. Though they faced severe persecution from Jews and Romans, the letter of James was a stark reminder that they could walk in victory if they would set their minds upon Christ and not allow themselves to be conformed to the world. That message still resonates today. His letter of instructions to the Church remains timeless, a needed reminder that everyone will face many obstacles in life, but Jesus has given us a roadmap to victory.

It seems like a broken record to say that James is relentless as he continues to warn those who trust in their riches that a day of judgment is coming. Is it possible that these verses are warnings for that day as well as prophetic warnings of future events? I believe they are.

He warns the rich man who abuses, condemns, and puts to death the righteous man that his riches will not help him in the day of judgment. Jesus said, *"Again I say to you, it is easier for a camel to go through the eye of a needle, than for a rich man to enter the kingdom of God"* (Matt. 19:24). This is simply another way of saying that no amount of money can purchase one salvation ticket into heaven. That does not mean that God is against prosperity. In fact, it is just the opposite. Though Jesus warned about the love of money, He wants us to prosper for His Kingdom's sake.

It was not by accident that the Holy Spirit inspired the apostle John to write, *"Beloved, I pray that in all respects you may prosper and be in good health, just as your soul prospers"* (3 John 2). Being rich is not the issue. Lusting for riches is the issue. Lusting after riches is like cancer to the soul. Abraham, Isaac, and Jacob were all very wealthy, and Jesus said concerning them, *"I say to you that many will come from east and west, and recline at the table with Abraham, Isaac and Jacob in the kingdom of heaven"* (Matt. 8:11). God is not opposed to the rich, but He is very opposed to the proud. Proverbs 10:22 declares, *"It is the blessing of the Lord that makes rich, and He adds no sorrow to it."* Such is not the case with those whose life-long goal is to accumulate wealth.

James could not have known how prophetic his words concerning the miseries of the rich would turn out to be. In AD 70, a Roman general named Titus marched against Israel and laid siege to the city of Jerusalem. The city itself was laid waste, and thousands upon thousands of Jews died at the hands of the Romans. When Titus left, there were no rich men. Those who survived were equally poor, their wealth no longer existed.

Jesus did know what the future held, so He told a parable about a rich man who decided to build bigger barns instead of using his blessings to help others. He called that man a fool because he errantly trusted in his riches, not knowing that he would be lying in a grave before his barns were completed. He was not a fool because he lacked knowledge. God called him a fool because he trusted in his riches.

Vs. 7-8: *⁷ Therefore be patient, brethren, until the coming of the Lord. The farmer waits for the precious produce of the soil, being patient about it, until it gets the early and late rains. ⁸ You too be patient; strengthen your hearts, for the coming of the Lord is near.*

Patience and long suffering are not attributes that come naturally or easily to most of us. We have become accustomed to cell phones, drive-thru windows, and microwave ovens, but Jesus said that is not the way His Kingdom operates. Jesus taught us saying, *"The soil produces crops by itself; first the blade, then the head, then the mature grain in the head"* (Mark 4:28).

Only mature Christians are capable of exuding patience, and they would be quick to remind others that patience is never gained by pleasing the flesh. When is the last time we heard a message on fasting? Jesus said, *"When you pray"* (Matt. 6:6), and He also said, *"Whenever you fast"* (Matt. 6:16). He did not say "if," so we can safely conclude that prayer and fasting should be a normal part of our Christian walk.

A wonderful friend tried to persuade me that there is no need to fast because we are now under the new covenant of grace. I sincerely wish I could find Scripture to affirm such theology, but as of this writing, I have been unable to do so. However, anyone who says they love to fast, and I am sure there are such Christians, are light years ahead of most of us. Even so, we should always strive to make fasting an integral part of our spiritual walk. Fasting denies the flesh and has a way of causing our patience and faith to increase dramatically.

It is in the moments when we are striving for a breakthrough, when nothing seems to be happening, and our prayers seem to be unanswered that we become willing to surrender and allow God to teach us patience. When we have sown seeds of faith and still do not see the wanted results, we must remember that the ground is busily supplying nutrients and supplements to the seed. In the same way, God is always attentive to our prayers, and He is not trying to decide if the answer is "Yes" or "No." That decision was made in the beginning and purchased yet again at the Cross. His answer is always "yes" when we pray according to His will. Therefore, we are not to lose hope, but we are to wait and trust in faith. Patience will be the result.

Vs. 9-11: *⁹Do not complain, brethren, against one another, so that you yourselves may not be judged; behold, the Judge is standing at the door. ¹⁰As an example, brethren, of suffering and patience, take the prophets who spoke in the name of the Lord. ¹¹We count those blessed who endured. You have heard of the endurance of Job and have seen the outcome of the Lord's dealing, that the Lord is full of compassion and is merciful.*

We may get the feeling that James has earned a Ph.D. in stepping on toes, but he is actually a very loving man of God who is genuinely concerned for the welfare of all God's children. Once again, he uses the term "brethren" as a reminder that he is not aloof to their trials and temptations. If they were being persecuted, he even more, but he steadfastly refused to allow his circumstances to prevail and steal his joy, as well as God's perfect plan for his life.

When God repeats Himself and again warns us against judging others, (see verse nine), we would be wise to pay close attention. Scripture tells us to pray for our enemies, and we will cause burning coals to be heaped upon their heads. The burning coals represent the power of the Holy Spirit to convict and draw people back to God. James warns about the evil of judging others because he has seen how the enemy is able to use it against us.

Perhaps you have noticed that judging others is a close friend of gossip. In other words, one sin leads to another. We can easily defuse the temptation to participate in judging others by taking the offense. It is amazing how fast the atmosphere changes when we say something like, "It sounds like they need prayer, so let's just stop and pray a blessing over them." This is a tried and proven method of placing Jesus on His rightful throne and dethroning the enemy.

In verse eleven, James began a church tradition when He picked Job as his subject for teaching patience. Since that time, "The Patience of Job" has been preached in almost every church in existence, with Job being the one person above all others who exemplified patience, and for good reason. No one had more reason to be upset with an angry wife and so-called well meaning friends than Job. His wife encouraged him to curse God and die, while his friends continually accused him of hidden sin, believing that the terrible things that occurred were the result of God's judgment.

Misunderstanding of the Book of Job has allowed our enemy to invoke an erroneous mindset that crosses over denominational lines. That mindset is that God is still judging His children. Such is not the case. God did allow Satan to try the faith of Job, but it was not God that reaped havoc on Job, it was Satan. Under the Old Covenant, God did at various times judge and execute judgment, but the war between God and man ceased when Jesus took all judgment on Himself on the Cross. The war between God and man is over! He is no longer holding our sins against us. Hebrews 10:17, *"And their sins and their lawless deeds I will remember no more."*

In the case of Job, the Bible clearly reveals that the evil came from the ploys of Satan, not from God. God had placed a hedge of protection around Job that Satan could not penetrate. Guess what? He has placed a strong hedge of protection around you and me as well. Satan was able to break through Job's hedge of protection because of Job's fear. Job lived in constant fear that his children were sinning against God (Job 3:25), and they probably were. His fear, however, proved to be counter-productive to his faith, which in turn left an opening in his hedge of protection. Unlike God's people after the coming of the Holy Spirit, Job did not have the ability to hear Satan's request that God allow Job to be tested. And it is unlikely that it would have changed the outcome if he had.

News Flash! God still allows Satan to test His children. God will not tempt us, but He will allow us to be tempted. With every temptation comes a time of testing. What will we do? Give in to our flesh, or stand on God's Word? Thankfully, we have a far greater covenant than did Job. We have the power of the Holy Spirit living in us. Job did not. Therefore, Job said concerning all the terrible things that happened, *"The Lord gave and the Lord has taken away. Blessed be the name of the Lord"* (Job 1:21).

Unfortunately, countless numbers of Christians have bought into the words of Job instead of the words of our Lord. Job should have said, "God gives and makes a way."

Am I saying that God never gives and takes away? No,

God is still in the business of giving and taking away, but He is not giving us sickness and poverty to teach us something. Granted, we usually learn a lot more when things are not going well, but that is because we do not seem to stay as close to God when our lives are thriving in prosperity. If we truly believe that it is God who has afflicted us with sickness, then we would have to conclude that sickness is His will for us. Why then would we go to a doctor to get well if it is His will for us to be sick? Only religion can come up with such wayward thinking. This is a good time for many to get this revelation: **God wants us well!** So then, how does God give and take away? He gives salvation to anyone who will receive His Son Jesus as Savior, and at the moment of our rebirth, He takes away our sins.

Vs. 12: *¹² But above all, my brethren, do not swear, either by heaven or by earth or with any other oath; but your yes is to be yes, and your no, no, so that you may not fall under judgment.*

James now completes the warning he began in Chapter 4, verses 13 through 17. He warns us that it is sinful to presume on tomorrow and make promises we may not be able to keep. He is not saying that we should never take an oath or make a vow. If that was His intent, we would never hear vows and oaths taken in courtrooms or weddings. He is simply saying that we should not take an oath or make promises concerning things that we have no control over. God is saying, "Let our yes be 'yes' and our no, 'no'." We should always strive to keep our word. It is sin to tell someone we will do something and not do everything in our power to keep our word.

When my wife and I were young parents, there were times when our children would beg me to stop what I was doing and play with them. On many occasions, I would conveniently put them off by promising to do it later. Do you know what a child never forgets? They never forget a promise that mom or dad makes. My wife told me more than once, "You promised the children …" I hate to admit it, but at that point in life, I had very little patience, and to make matters worse, I had not harnessed my anger. When my wife pressed me about keeping my word, my anger button was not hard to find. There were times when the lid blew, and out spewed unkind words. Not curse words, but unkind words that still had the power to hurt. Then I was twice guilty. But I give thanks to my loving wife and heavenly Father that I have been able to raise my level of integrity to a higher level. I have not arrived, but I have pushed off from shore.

Today, I am slow to make a promise, and I rarely become angry. When I do make a promise, I make every effort to keep it. Making a promise and keeping our word is of vital importance because it reveals who we really are. When we intentionally fail to keep our word, we are in danger of tarnishing both our name and the name of our good Father. God always keeps His promises, and He expects us to do the same. Proverbs 22:1, *"A good name is to be more desired than great wealth."*

Vs. 13-15: *¹³Is anyone among you suffering? Then he must pray. Is anyone cheerful? He is to sing praises. ¹⁴ Is anyone among you sick? Then he must call for the elders of the church and they are to pray over him, anointing him with oil in the name of the Lord; ¹⁵ and the prayer offered in faith will restore the one who is sick, and the Lord will raise him up, and if he has committed sins, they will be forgiven him.*

James has already declared that all good gifts come from above and bad gifts do not, and that should settle the issue. Unfortunately, for many in the body of Christ, it does not. When we get confused over Scripture or doctrine, we should immediately go to the four gospel accounts for answers. Although God is alive in every book of the Bible, it is in the gospels that we see Him more clearly because it is there that His Son walked the earth in the flesh. Jesus said to Phillip, *"He who has seen Me has seen the Father"* (John 14:9).

Sound doctrine demands that the epistles give testimony to the gospels, and they do exactly that. When we find a Scripture that seems hard to understand, it is usually a Scripture verse found in one of the epistles, such as the apostle Paul's thorn in the flesh. Beware! Several doctrines have emerged in various denominations that are based on misunderstood Scripture. Paul's thorn in the flesh is one of those. Who gave Paul a thorn in the flesh? Second Corinthians 12:7, *"There was given me a thorn in the flesh, a messenger of Satan to torment* [persecute] *me" (bracketed words added).*

God allowed Satan to torment Paul, but God was not

the Author of the torment. Everywhere Paul went to preach the Gospel of Grace, Jews who hated the grace gospel followed him. Because of them, Paul suffered thirty-nine lashes of the whip on five different occasions. Three times he was beaten with rods, and once he was stoned and left for dead. Even as we pray when we are beset by troubles, so did the apostle Paul. He prayed not once, but three different times that God would remove his thorn. What was God's reply? *"My Grace is sufficient for you"* (verse 9). In other words, God told Paul that He would not remove persecution, but He would be Paul's strength and take him through the persecution. Tongue in cheek, all of us wish we could avoid Satan's persecution and harassment, but God knows best. When He returns, He will deal a death blow to our tormentor, Satan. Until then, His grace is sufficient for us as well.

We could move on from the subject of suffering and let the above commentary suffice, but I feel led to take this subject a little deeper. Let me reiterate that God still allows His children to suffer from persecution, but He is not the One who brings persecution. If we suffer from persecution, God will either take us through or help us to endure. One thing is for sure, He will never leave us nor forsake us (see Matt. 28:20).

Pain and suffering is not always rooted in persecution, but persecution is always rooted in Satan's attempt to keep the gospel of Christ from being heard. There is pain and suffering all around us. Go to any doctor's office or hospital, and we will see firsthand those who are enduring pain and suffering. Perhaps, dear reader, you are at this very minute going through pain and suffering. Perhaps it is physical, perhaps it is circumstances, perhaps it is the result of a broken marriage or some other type of broken relationship. Whatever it is, God wants to free you from pain and suffering.

Let's look together at three major sources that cause pain and suffering.

#1 – The first is Satan. He is constantly looking for someone to devour, especially Christians. Those who lack knowledge of God's Word and how God's Kingdom operates are easy targets to be enveloped in doubt, worry, and fear.

#2 – The second reason we suffer is because of Adam's original sin. When sin came, the curse came with it, causing us to be born into a fallen world. People fall, and when they do, they tend to get hurt. Driving too fast or falling asleep at the steering wheel has resulted in many life-changing injuries and deaths, but we are foolish if we blame God when those things happen. Physical laws, such as the Law of Gravity and the Law of Force, treat everyone the same.

#3 – The third way that suffering finds its way into our lives is because "we make bad decisions." Again, we must remind ourselves that our failure to seek God's direction for every facet of our lives is a recipe for disaster. For instance, God will not lead us into debt, but many people are miserably in debt because they failed to seek God's counsel before they bought things they could not afford. God will not lead us to have sex outside of marriage, but many have ignored His command and have suffered the consequences of doing so.

Good news! No matter the source, no matter the amount of suffering that comes into our lives, our God is more than willing to deliver us from it. His direction for getting deliverance is simple. We are instructed to pray and seek His wisdom concerning our need for help! Once we have committed our needs to the Lord, our part is to believe that God has granted our request. Jesus said, *"all things for which you pray and ask, believe that you have received them, and they will be granted you"* (Mark 11:24). God did not make freedom from suffering complicated.

It is wonderful that James admonishes the cheerful brethren to sing praises unto the Lord. Demons want to bombard our minds and keep us focused on suffering and loss. The Holy Spirit wants us to focus on cheerfulness and gain. Both are mindsets, but only one is beneficial. Nothing stops the assault of the enemy faster than voicing words, songs, and praises unto the Lord.

In verse fourteen, James gives instructions concerning the sick. To say the least, the doctrine of healing varies from denomination to denomination. Some believe that healing is for today, some do not, and some do not know what they believe. As we move forward on this subject, let me repeat the advice given earlier: "Take what you can eat and leave the rest for someone else."

James is not saying that calling for the Elders and anointing the sick with oil is the only way that the sick are healed, and he is not saying that everyone will always be healed. He said, "The prayer offered in faith will raise them up." Is it always necessary for Elders to pray for the sick? No, but that is one way, and it is a good one. The Book of Acts bears witness that believing God and speaking His name works for the entire body of Christ. So why does James say to send the Elders to pray over the sick? The apparent answer lies in the fact that these men of position should be grounded in God's Word and not easily moved by sight and circumstances.

James directed the elders to anoint the sick with oil. Oil was a key ingredient used to heal sores and infections during the days of James' ministry. Therefore, it did have a positive influence on those who were sick, but that was not the real reason James directed elders and deacons to anoint the sick with oil. Oil is symbolic of the Holy Spirit, the Third Person of the Trinity. We should take careful notice also that James did not say, "If it is God's will, the sick person will be healed." He said, the prayer offered in "faith" will raise him up. Dear brothers and sisters, we can anoint the sick with oil until they slide off the bed, but healing will not manifest unless faith is involved. Thankfully, there are times when God chooses to circumvent all of our beliefs and unbeliefs and perform a miracle, not because of us, but in spite of us. However, those times are not the norm. The bottom line is this: we cannot put God into our little belief box and expect Him to stay there.

I have emphasized the need for faith because faith is important, but we should not become errant fools concerning the issue of faith. First of all, God will never give us faith to believe something that is not in His will. A dear sister of the faith told me that early in her Christian walk she was attempting to glean and increase her faith in the area of healing. As she sought truth concerning healing knowledge, she thought she heard God tell her to take a friend and pray over a dearly departed loved one. They stood over the casket of the deceased and prayed, commanded, and demanded, but nothing happened. The dearly departed remained in the state of the departed. They felt as though they had failed, and they had, but not because that person was not brought back to life. They failed because they confused their flesh with the voice of God. God will never send us anywhere to fail. He is not in the failing business.

Are people still raised from the dead? Yes. There are many documented cases of the dead being raised. Concerning such miracles, Jesus said, *"Truly, truly, I say to you, he who believes in Me, the works that I do, he will do also; and greater works than these he will do; because I go to the Father"* (John 14:12). What are the greater works? There is much debate concerning the greater works, but most Christians have not even seen the works that He did accomplished in their lives, much less the greater works.

I have seen healing miracles and can therefore testify in truth that healing is for today. At the same time, I readily confess that I have not seen healing miracles that I desired to see. God quickly taught me not to take credit when healing does occur, but equally as important, He taught me to not take credit when healing does not occur. I have no healing power, as in none, nada, zero. All healing comes from the Father. Let me also add that all healing emanates from the divine nature of God. God is looking for faith but not blind faith. As one praise song says, "It's not over if God is in it." At the same time, when God is not in it, the show is over and the stage curtain has been drawn.

As to the greater works, (this is 1st Griffin), I believe that the greater works is not a healing of the body but a leading of lost souls into the Kingdom of God. Everyone is welcome to meditate on that for themselves. Yet, God's Word declares, *"There is an appointed time for everything. And there is a time for every event under heaven—a time to give birth, and a time to die"* (Eccl. 3:1-2).

That is God's Word, and it is unchanging. But we should bear in mind that death was not a part of God's original plan for mankind. Adam and Eve were created to live forever, but when sin came, death followed. The apostle Paul confirms God's promise that in the day Adam ate of the tree of the knowledge of good and evil, he would die, as he writes in Romans 8:10, *"the body is dead because of sin."* Nothing can change that truth. Unless Christ calls His Church first, we will all die, but our physical death will have no power over our spiritual souls. At the sound of the trumpet, Christ will call His Church from this earth with a shout, and the dead in Christ, as well as believers who are still living, will exchange their mortal bodies for immortal bodies, the perishable for the imperishable. Until then, we must all deal with the issue of death. Take it to the bank, when the day that God has appointed for us to die arrives, no one's faith will extend that time for even one millisecond.

Earlier in my Christian walk, I would enter a sickroom with one thing in mind, and that was to get the sick person well. God began to show me that some people had lived their lives, and their appointed time had come. I have also learned, when possible, to ask the sick if they want to be healed. At times, I find that some do not want to be healed. They have fought the fight of faith and are ready to go home and be with the Lord.

Jesus found a man lying at the Pool of Bethesda who had been sick for thirty-eight years and asked, *"Do you wish to get well?"* (John 5:6). We may find it hard to understand, but there are people who love their infirmities. You know, the ones you ask, "How are you doing?" and find that you have opened a floodgate to misery and its love for company.

Finally, James did not err in his assessment of how the sick are to be healed. He was spot on. When faith meets faith, the divine power of the Almighty will intercede, and this we know, something good is about to happen.

Vs. 16: *¹⁶ Therefore, confess your sins to one another, and pray for one another so that you may be healed. The effective prayer of a righteous man can accomplish much.*

A wise person will take into consideration the fullness of God's Word concerning the confession of sins to others. God has already forgiven our sins, but that is not what James is referring to in these verses. Let me add that there is an inherent danger in taking this verse out of context as a pretext for doctrine. If we have sinned against others, then we should be willing to ask for their forgiveness and attempt to reconcile our differences with them. If they refuse to accept our offer of forgiveness, they are the ones that remain in bondage, not us. God will not lead us to share intimate things with a pastor, elder, or anyone else unless they can be trusted to keep our confidence.

However, there may be a time when the Holy Spirit instructs us to confess a sin or sins with another person, or persons, or openly with the entire Church body. To that, we need to be obedient, but again we should be sure that it is the Holy Spirit prompting us and not a strange voice. Those we share with should also be known prayer warriors, men and women who will pray and believe for victory over bondage, sin, and sickness.

There was a young doctor in our congregation who was led by the Holy Spirit to testify before the Church that he had been held in bondage to pornography for many years but that God had delivered him. The enemy would have loved to use his testimony against him, but because it was Spirit-led the enemy had to stand aside. His testimony gave to him a newfound freedom, but it blessed the Church and offered hope to others as well.

James reminds us that we are righteous in the eyes of God. For many Christians, that is a hard pill to swallow because we are continually taught that we are nothing but "old sinners saved by grace." It sounds pious, but it is no longer true. We were old sinners, and we were saved by grace, but it is also true that a great exchange was made when we became born-again believers. God took our sin and gave us His righteousness (see 2 Cor. 5:21). Therefore, we can now enter the throne room of grace with the full knowledge that God is not rejecting our prayers.

Vs. 17-18: *¹⁷ Elijah was a man with a nature like ours, and he prayed earnestly that it would not rain, and it did not rain on the earth for three years and six months. Then he prayed again, and the sky poured rain and the earth produced its fruit.*

James looked into the annals of Jewish history to once again remind us that God is no respecter of persons. Most of us have no trouble looking at Elijah and believing that

God would answer his prayers because he was a prophet. We look at ourselves and think, *I am not a prophet and God has never used me to perform a miracle.* That is the natural mindset of the average Christian, but we should bear in mind that neither Elijah, nor Paul, nor anyone else had the ability to perform a miracle. God performed the miracles through them because they were willing vessels, and they were full of faith. He will do the same through us if we will make ourselves available.

We serve the same God who is more than willing to do miracles through us. Elijah had the anointing of the Holy Spirit, but James reminds us that he had a "nature like ours." How much more should we be able to allow God's miracle-working power to flow through us because we have the Holy Spirit living inside us. Our part is to be obedient and believe that He who called us is faithful to watch over His spoken Word.

Vs. 19-20: *¹⁹ My brethren, if any among you strays from the truth and one turns him back, ²⁰ let him know that he who turns a sinner from the error of his way will save his soul from death and will cover a multitude of sins.*

James ends his letter by making a final call to the brethren to walk in fulfillment of the Law of Liberty (unconditional love). These verses are not about losing our salvation (position) in Christ, but they have everything to do with losing our relationship with Him. God wants us to reach out in love and not shun Christians who are not walking in a way that is pleasing to Christ. It is very easy and tempting to write someone off because they are in some type of sin that we find to be offensive. Before crossing that bridge, we should prayerfully consider that we may be the only mediator left that is willing to petition heaven on their behalf.

Jesus is our Good Shepherd, but He has called us to be sheepherders. Many of those who are straying from the flock will, in time, repent as they are brought to remembrance of who they are and Whose they are, allowing God's grace to cover a multitude of sins.

EPILOGUE

I pray that you have enjoyed your study of the rich Book of James. As we have discovered, it is full of practical, godly wisdom that makes it as relevant today as it was the day it was written by James. His warnings are still relevant, His instructions for guarding our tongues are still relevant, and His instructions on living moral, productive lives are still relevant.

We may ask ourselves, "How often did I find that the Holy Spirit was bringing conviction to me as I studied the Book of James?" I cannot speak for others, but it seems the writer had me in mind as God inspired him to write his letter to the Church. I cannot, in truth, say that I count it all joy when trials and troubles come my way. I certainly cannot say that I have conquered my tongue. And I was forced to plead "guilty in the first-degree" concerning favoritism of some over others. Last, but certainly not least, the entire Church is forced to take an inward look when James exclaims, "faith without works is dead," the centerpiece of the entire Book (see James 2:26).

Still, we would be amiss if we were to end this study with a negative view of ourselves. We all study God's Word because we love our Lord, and we love His Word. For this we know, "He who began a good work in you will perfect it until the day of Jesus Christ." We are all a work in progress.

OTHER BOOKS BY

DON GRIFFIN

"Great Life, Great Marriage"

God's "can't miss" plan to understanding how the Kingdom of God operates for success in every area of your life.

- Are you ready to experience God's best and to move into the supernatural where miracles and abundance are the norm?
- Are you ready to let God remove every shackle, every chain, every encumbrance and to begin walking in the Law of Liberty?
- Are you ready to let God have control of every area of your life?

If you really have a burning desire to change your present circumstances or your environment, you can. "Great Life, Great Marriage" reveals God's biblical can't-miss plan for an exciting, fruitful life and a fun-filled marriage.

This book is a must read!

Available through Amazon and most retailers.

Don and Penny Griffin

ABOUT THE AUTHOR

DONALD GRIFFIN was born in a small South Georgia town. He is a seasoned businessman with a heart for writing and teaching the Word of God. Although his parents had very little formal education, they instilled in him three very important priorities for life: the Bible, prayer, and church. As a result, he accepted Christ at the early age of twelve. At the age of seventeen, Don joined the United States Air Force with the intention of seeing the world. Instead, he was stationed in South Carolina, less than three hundred miles from his home, and stayed there until his discharge.

Don remained in South Carolina for the next ten years. During that time, he married, fathered three sons, and became a successful farmer of more than fifteen hundred acres of land. He and his family attended a small Methodist church where he taught a young couples' class and filled the pulpit when the pastor was away. Characterized by a lifestyle of seeking both the trappings of the world and the things of the Kingdom, his life began to slowly unravel. The cost was high, and at the age of thirty-three, Don had lost his marriage, his sons, and his business. He decided to return to his roots in South Georgia and found the long trip back home to be one of the most lonely, heartbreaking times of his life. Back home in Georgia, Don rededicated his life to the Lord Jesus but struggled to restart his business career.

It was during this time of his life that Don met a beautiful young lady named Sarah Penny Mixon who owned and operated a very successful dance studio. Penny was also a casualty of divorce but was blessed to have exited her broken marriage with a precious daughter. Don and Penny soon married, and two years later, Penny gave birth to their son.

Don continued to struggle in his efforts to establish his own business but rediscovered that God has a way of placing the right people into one's life when their trust is in Him. A successful insurance businessman came into his life and helped him establish an insurance agency of his own. Griffin Insurance Agency in Douglas, Georgia, was born. The early years were very difficult, but Don and Penny had learned that tough times have the power to build you up or tear you down. After much prayer, Penny made a decision to leave her own business and help her husband complete his dream.

About The Author

Hard work and perseverance have rewarded them with a very successful Insurance Agency.

Don is now semi-retired and enjoys a great relationship with the love of his life, Penny, and all of their children. He is a living testimony that God can take a broken life and put it back together. Don and Penny are active in their church and enjoy teaching and ministering the uncompromised Word of God into the lives of His people.

You can find more of Don's teachings at their website:
www.DonAndPenny.com

Don may be reached via email at:
don@griffinagency.com

www.ingramcontent.com/pod-product-compliance
Lightning Source LLC
LaVergne TN
LVHW051843080426
835512LV00018B/3036